AMERICA'S MARY

The Story of Our Lady of Good Help

Marge Steinhage Fenelon

Our Sunday Visitor
Huntington, Indiana

Nihil Obstat
Msgr. Michael Heintz, Ph.D.
Censor Librorum

Imprimatur
✠ Kevin C. Rhoades
Bishop of Fort Wayne-South Bend
February 25, 2022

The *Nihil Obstat* and *Imprimatur* are official declarations that a book is free from doctrinal or moral error. It is not implied that those who have granted the *Nihil Obstat* and *Imprimatur* agree with the contents, opinions, or statements expressed.

Our Sunday Visitor Publishing Division, Our Sunday Visitor, Inc., 200 Noll Plaza, Huntington, IN 46750; www.osv.com; 1-800-348-2440
ISBN: 978-1-68192-341-3 (Inventory No. T2023)
1. RELIGION—History.
2. RELIGION—Christianity—Saints & Sainthood.
3. RELIGION—Christianity—Catholic.
eISBN: 978-1-68192-342-0
LCCN: 2022934999

Cover design: Tyler Ottinger
Cover art: Courtesy of the National Shrine of Our Lady of Good Help
Interior design: Amanda Falk

PRINTED IN THE UNITED STATES OF AMERICA

To the Queen of Heaven

CONTENTS

PREFACE

I learned of the apparition of Our Lady of Good Help in 2010, when I was asked by the *National Catholic Register* to cover the apparition's decree of authenticity by the bishop of the Diocese of Green Bay, Bishop David L. Ricken. Like the vast majority of other Catholics, I had never heard of Our Lady of Good Help, nor was I aware that there was a Church-approved Marian apparition site in Champion, Wisconsin, just two hours from my home. I was delighted to take on the assignment and to dig deeper into the little-known story of how Mary appeared to Adele Brise in the wild woods of Wisconsin's Door Peninsula in 1859.

Writing that article awakened in me a longing to spend more time at the apparition site, and I began to make regular pilgrimages to the National Shrine of Our Lady of Good Help. I wrote more articles about this fascinating and holy place and included a chapter on it in my book, *My Queen, My Mother: A Marian Pilgrimage Across America*. I have loved the inexplicable peacefulness that prevails, no matter what event is being held or how many pilgrims are on the property. There could be busloads of people, and you would never know it because all is enveloped in the peace and presence of the Queen of Heaven, as she called herself during the apparitions. Nearly everyone who visits experiences this same sense of peace, and this has become recognized as one of the shrine's main characteristics. No one fully understands it, but everyone notices and cherishes it. Had it not been for that *National Catholic Register* article, I would never have discovered it myself.

Mary keeps calling me back to Champion, and so it was easy for me to accept when Our Sunday Visitor asked me to write a book about the apparition of Our Lady of Champion. The complete story must be told, and people must learn about the only Church-approved Marian apparition on United States soil. The message Mary gave to Adele Brise was meant for all of us: Do penance, sacrifice, receive the sacraments frequently, and teach the children their catechism. It's part of our American Catholic heritage and our mission as Catholic Americans. Our country needs the message and mission of Our Lady of Champion now more than ever!

The past three years of writing this book have been difficult in so very many ways. The content itself was a challenge because of the research involved and the amount of time it took to sort and compile it. Trips back and forth to the shrine, archives to sift through, interviews to conduct, and maps to examine, all required much of me. Some of the history of the Belgian people, the apparitions, and the chapel was passed down orally through generations and written down at later dates or from secondhand knowledge. This meant cross-checking sources and countless journeys down rabbit holes to piece details together. In a few cases, exact details could not be verified, and these have been noted in the book.

In between all of that, God sent some unusually heavy crosses for me to bear, and allowed the most vicious spiritual warfare I've ever experienced to affect not only me, but my entire family. At one point, it became necessary to lay the manuscript aside for a time and tend to these urgent spiritual matters. Despite all of that, I never faltered in my conviction that Mary wanted me to tell the story and that she would somehow see me through it.

She did see me through, and the book you hold in your hands is proof of that. I owe a debt of gratitude to Our Lady for her guidance and protection, to Adele Brise for her intercession, and to Our Sunday Visitor for their unfailing support and encouragement.

Marge Steinhage Fenelon

INTRODUCTION

By Michael O'Neill

It seems that devotees to different titles of the Virgin Mary have hometown connections much like fans of baseball or soccer teams by city, region, and country. You might encounter a Catholic from Latin America — whether it be from México with a love for Our Lady of Guadalupe, or Cuba with Our Lady of Charity of El Cobre, or the Dominican Republic with Our Lady of Altagracia — or a follower of any of the myriad other titles of Mary from traditionally Catholic localities that confirms this fact. With the seemingly endless number of different titles of the Virgin Mary remembered in miracle accounts, festivals, feast days, canonical coronations, and the laying of cornerstones of shrines big and small worldwide, the words of a traditional Flemish hymn ring evermore true: Love gave her a thousand names.

With every Christian country comes at least one famous Marian title almost as assuredly as there is a flag for that nation. The United States is somewhat different, however, where Catholics might be attracted to Mary's sobriquets connected to the nationalities of their families of origin, or have found a spiritual home with one of the most widely celebrated miraculous titles of Mary: Our Lady of Fatima, Our Lady of Lourdes, or Our Lady of Mt. Carmel. It begs the question: Where is "America's Mary"?

The patroness of the Americas is of course Our Lady of Guadalupe, and the United States is consecrated to Mary, the Immaculate Conception, with the National Basilica bearing that title. (It was also the original name of the Mississippi River.) There have been exactly four canonical coronations by the Vatican of Marian images in the history of the United States:

- Our Lady of Prompt Succor (New Orleans, Louisiana, 1895)
- Our Lady of Mount Carmel (New York City, 1905)
- Our Lady of the Immaculate Conception (Lake Charles, Louisiana, 2013)
- Our Lady of La Leche (St. Augustine, Florida, 2021)

But only Catholic trivia buffs could easily rattle off that list, and each of those special events is only celebrated locally. They have not made it into the hearts and consciousness of American Catholics at large.

And while the highly honored Marian statues in New Orleans and St. Augustine have a reputation for being associated with miracles, phenomena of other sorts that have been frequently reported and occasionally validated by ecclesiastical authorities in other countries — namely, Marian apparitions and weeping statues or icons — have been beyond rare in the history of the relatively young United States. Such supernatural occurrences fall in the realm of private revelation, so it is possible to be a faithful Catholic and ignore these messages and de-emphasize them, for they "do not belong … to the deposit of faith" (CCC 67). But for miracle-minded Catholics and those with strong Marian devotion, many are curious about the history and status of such happenings.

Perhaps the first case of a reported Marian apparition in the territory that would become the United States (aside from a legendary appearance of the Virgin Mary to George Washington at Valley Forge in 1777) was on Christmas Eve 1841 in Montana's Bitterroot Valley. It is said that Mary appeared to an eleven-year-old boy named Paul from the Salish Native American people as he prepared for the sacraments with Father Pierre-Jean De Smet and the Jesuit missionaries there. Since that time, in the twentieth century and beyond, there have been 122 cases of alleged Marian apparitions publicly reported in the United States. Most of these cases were ignored by Catholic Church authorities and went uninvestigated, with a very small number of instances, like Nancy Fowler (Conyers, Georgia, 1990), receiving an official judgment of *non constat de supernaturalitate* (Latin for "not established as supernatural") — meaning that there wasn't enough evidence at that time to declare them miraculous, but leaving the case open in a "wait-and-see" status. (Currently any such American cases from that period appear to be closed and not likely to be re-opened.) Similarly, in a judgment in more recent times, the popular Our Lady of America visions reported by Sr. Mildred Mary Neuzil (Rome City, Indiana, 1956) were judged by pertinent local authorities on May 7, 2020, not to have a supernatural character.

Some cases at the end of the twentieth century were given the Church's most negative judgment *constat de non supernaturalitate* (Latin for "established as not supernatural"), such as the alleged visions of Gianna Talone Sullivan (Scottsdale, Arizona,

1988, and Emmittsburg, Maryland, 1994). This judgment was the same sort as the highly publicized condemned cases of Mary Van Hoof (Necedah, WI, 1949) and Veronica Leuken (Bayside, New York, 1970) in previous decades.

Into the twenty-first century, never in the history of the United States had there been a Marian apparition judged positively by the local bishop — the competent authority in the judgment of cases of private revelation outlined in the Vatican's 1978 rule book "Norms Regarding the Manner of Proceeding in the Discernment of Presumed Apparitions or Revelations" — and classified as *constat de supernaturalitate* (Latin for "established as supernatural").

This all changed, however, on December 8, 2010 in Champion, at the (now National) Shrine of Our Lady of Good Help. Bishop David L. Ricken of the Diocese of Green Bay gave his historic approval of the three apparitions reported in 1859, less than two decades after the first reported apparition in the United States, and one year after the famed visions of Our Lady of Lourdes to fourteen-year-old Bernadette Soubirous. In Robinsonville, Wisconsin, a twenty-eight-year-old Belgian immigrant named Adele Brise saw a beautiful woman dressed in dazzling white with a golden sash. A church was built there, at Mary's request, and the visionary took the words of the Virgin Mary to heart: "Gather the children in this wild country and teach them what they should know for salvation." Adele did what she could to dedicate her life to the fulfillment of the Virgin Mary's request, volunteering to clean people's homes in exchange for a chance to teach children their catechism, how to make the Sign of the Cross, and how to approach the sacraments.

Twelve years later, on the same night as the Great Chicago Fire, the 1871 Fire ravaged Wisconsin. The fires were said to have approached the edges of the church property in Champion (the name after Robinsonville), but the church itself was amongst the grounds that were miraculously spared. That night Our Lady of Good Help had answered the prayers of the faithful who processed with a Marian statue around the chapel. It is a miracle that is annually celebrated even today at the shrine, and perhaps was a key event that led the way to the apparition's historic approval.

As it turned out, the Great Fire Miracle was only the first of many miracles to happen at the shrine. Almost universally, pilgrims seem to experience a sense of peace walking in the footsteps of the Virgin Mary, and many medical healings have been claimed since the earliest days following the visions, as testified in documents and by crutches adorning the walls of the crypt of the shrine church.

This renown for miracles and the recognition of this place of grace as a national shrine invites us to approach Mary on pilgrimage there and grow closer to her and her Son through her intercession. Our Lady of Good Help is very clearly "America's Mary," and her message of catechizing the young rings truer even today than when the messages were first delivered in the "wild country" in 1859.

Yet the title of Our Lady of Good Help is still generally unknown to Catholics in the Unites States, and much work needs to be done to bring her message and mission to the fore. This powerful new book by Marge Steinhage Fenelon, *America's Mary: The Story of Our Lady of Good Help*, steps boldly into that void as she sheds light on Mary's ongoing maternity in the lives of all believers and connects us to the Mother of God made manifest in the events of 1859 in the farmland of Wisconsin. With her insights into Marian devotional life and presentation of the historical foundations for our understanding of Mary's unique role in salvation history, we can confidently and proudly embrace Our Lady of Good Help as "America's Mary."

Chapter One

APPARITION OR IMAGINATION?

When the Blessed Virgin Mary appeared to Lucia dos Santos and her cousins Jacinta and Francisco Marto at Fátima in 1917, she revealed herself as Our Lady of the Rosary and made specific requests of the children for prayer, penance, sacrifice, and devotion to her Immaculate Heart. Sadly, their reports of the apparitions met with skepticism and criticism. At first, the shepherd children's stories were dismissed as childish imagination. But as they held to their accounts, they garnered ridicule from the townspeople — including members of their own families, even to the point of being accused of lying by Lucia's mother.[1] In fact, the three little ones were imprisoned by the town Administrator, who threatened them with torture, life imprisonment, and death if they did not confess that their story was a lie.[2] But they insisted that they were telling the truth. It took the famed Miracle of the Sun to fully convince the people of Fátima and the surrounding area that the apparitions were real. After a thorough Church investigation, the apparitions were finally approved in 1930. Since then, Fátima has become one of the most well-known and cherished Marian apparitions in the world.

America's First and Only Approved Marian Apparition

In 1859, a lesser known but equally important Marian apparition took place on the Door Peninsula of northeastern Wisconsin. There, Mary appeared three times to a young Belgian woman named Adele Brise. Mary identified herself as the Queen of Heaven and gave Adele instructions to teach the children their catechism, pray, do penance, sacrifice, and receive the sacraments frequently. As with the Fátima children, Adele initially met with skepticism, and during her lifetime underwent many trials, including persecution. Still, she maintained that she was telling the truth and courageously carried on the mission the Blessed Mother had given to her. Although the local folk accepted Adele's story as real, and a popular piety built up around Mary's appearances and messages, it wasn't until more than one hundred years later that the local bishop conducted a thorough investigation and, in 2010, approved the apparitions.

Why the Church Investigates Apparition Claims

Why must the Church investigate claims of apparitions, and why does it sometimes take so long to reach a definitive conclusion? To adequately answer that question, we need to look into the history of how miracle and apparition claims have been handled by the Church.

The baseline for the Church's discernment of miracles and apparitions was established by St. Paul in his First Letter to the

Thessalonians: "Do not quench the Spirit, do not despise prophesying, but test everything; hold fast what is good, abstain from every form of evil" (1 Thes 5:19–22). The First Letter of John counsels the faithful similarly:

> Beloved, do not believe every spirit, but test the spirits to see whether they are of God; for many false prophets have gone out into the world. By this you know the Spirit of God: every spirit which confesses that Jesus Christ has come in the flesh is of God, and every spirit which does not confess Jesus is not of God. This is the spirit of Antichrist, of which you heard that it was coming, and now it is in the world already. (4:1–3)

Both John and Paul's advice point to the fact that not every spirit is a good spirit. Thus when considering claims of miracles, locutions, visions, and apparitions, we must be clear on who or what it is with which we are dealing. Satan is a liar and will go to great lengths to deceive the faithful, even to the point of masquerading as something — or someone — good in order to achieve an evil goal.[3]

The Church teaches that there are three possible sources for such occurrences: God, man, and the devil. With his diabolical trickery, the devil can produce imaginative visions and false ecstasies; cure sicknesses that have diabolic origins; produce the stigmata; simulate miracles, levitation, and bilocation; make people or objects seem to disappear; cause a person to hear sounds or voices; or cause someone to speak in tongues. On the surface, all these things can appear good and godly, but what's behind them is evil. Satan seeks to distract us from the genuine teachings of the Church and cause confusion and doubt in our faith. He wants to coax us into beliefs and practices that will lead us further and further from the Truth. He hopes for a complete crisis of faith that will eventually lead us out of the Church and into his power and allegiance. Diabolic spirits cultivate confusion, anxiety, pride, vanity, indiscretion, obstinacy, morbidity, and despair. On the other hand, spirits that are of God foster humility, enlightenment, prudence, obedience, and peace.[4] The contrast of principles is vast and striking, but the signs used by the devil can mimic those used by God.

And so, when someone believes they have experienced an apparition, the Church must take meticulous care to assure that what was seen, perceived, and experienced had divine origins. It's the Church's grave responsibility to protect the deposit of faith and the authentic teachings of Jesus Christ. The power to judge such things was given to the Church by Jesus through the person of Pete

> And I tell you, you are Peter, and on this rock I will build my Church, and the powers of death shall not prevail against it. I will give you the keys of the kingdom of heaven, and whatever you bind on earth shall be bound in heaven, and whatever you loose on earth shall be loosed in heaven. (Matthew 16:18–19)

Classification and Approval of Apparitions

Apparitions are classified by the Church as private revelations. Even when they are officially approved, the faithful are not required to believe in them. As the *Catechism of the Catholic Church* tells us:

> Throughout the ages, there have been so-called "private" revelations, some of which have been recognized by the authority of the Church. They do not belong, however, to the deposit of faith. It is not their role to improve or complete Christ's definitive Revelation, but to help live

more fully by it in a certain period of history. Guided by the magisterium of the Church, the *sensus fidelium* knows how to discern and welcome in these revelations whatever constitutes an authentic call of Christ or his saints to the Church.

Christian faith cannot accept "revelations" that claim to surpass or correct the Revelation of which Christ is the fulfillment, as is the case in certain non-Christian religions and also in certain recent sects which base themselves on such "revelations." (67)

In other words, the content of private revelation must never detract from the authentic and formal teachings of the Catholic Church. Rather, it must serve to help us live that which the Church teaches — which is what Christ himself taught — more fully.

With these safeguards in place, the Church is prudently cautious in the approval process of apparitions. When an apparition is reported and investigated, it is classified in three ways. The first is "not worthy of belief," meaning that the miracle or apparition does not meet the requirements for approval. This could be for any number of reasons, but the ultimate reason is to protect the faithful from being led astray. The second classification is "not contrary to the Faith," which means that, while the apparition cannot be proven definitively given the current evidence, the investigators did not find anything in it contrary to Catholic teaching.[5]

During the Council of Trent (1545–63), the Church established the local bishop as the first and main authority in apparition cases:

And that these things may be the more faithfully observed, the holy Synod ordains, that no one be allowed to place, or cause to be placed, any unusual image, in any place, or church, howsoever exempted, except that image have been approved of by the bishop: also, that no new miracles are to be acknowledged, or new relics recognized, unless the said bishop has taken cognizance and approved thereof; who, as soon as he has obtained some certain information in regard to these matters, shall, after having taken the advice of theologians, and of other pious men, act therein as he shall judge to be consonant with truth and piety. But if any doubtful, or difficult abuse has to be extirpated; or, in fine, if any more grave question shall arise touching these matters, the bishop, before deciding the controversy, shall await the sentence of the metropolitan and of the bishops of the province, in a provincial Council; yet so, that nothing new, or that previously has not been usual in the Church, shall be resolved on, without having first consulted the most holy Roman Pontiff.[6]

Thus reports of apparitions and miracles must be reported to the bishop of the diocese (or in Eastern Catholic churches to the eparch of the eparchy) in which it occurred. When evaluating these happenings, bishops follow a specific set of guidelines:

- The facts in the case are free of error.
- The person(s) receiving the messages is/are psychologically balanced, honest, moral, sincere, and respectful of Church authority.
- Doctrinal errors are not attributed to God, Our Lady, or to a saint.
- Theological and spiritual doctrines presented are free of error.

- Moneymaking is not a motive involved in the events.
- Healthy religious devotion and spiritual fruits result, with no evidence of collective hysteria.

Based on these criteria, a bishop can judge that an apparition shows signs of being an authentic or genuinely miraculous intervention from heaven, that it's clearly not miraculous or there is insufficient evidence to determine this, or that it's not evident whether or not it is authentic.[7]

Once a Marian apparition is approved by the bishop, the faithful are free to venerate Mary publicly at that site. In his 2010 apostolic exhortation *Verbum Domini* ("The Word of God"), Pope Benedict XVI addressed the subject of private revelation:

> Ecclesiastical approval of a private revelation essentially means that its message contains nothing contrary to faith and morals. It is licit to make it public and the faithful are authorized to give to it their prudent adhesion. A private revelation can introduce new emphases, give rise to new forms of piety, or deepen older ones. It can have a certain prophetic character and can be a valuable aid for better understanding and living the Gospel at a certain time; consequently, it should not be treated lightly. It is a help which is proffered, but its use is not obligatory.[8]

Once the bishop has either granted or withheld approval of an apparition, canon law obliges the faithful to be obedient to the bishop's declaration:

> Conscious of their own responsibility, the Christian faithful are bound to follow with Christian obedience

those things which the sacred pastors, inasmuch as they represent Christ, declare as teachers of the faith or establish as rulers of the Church.[9]

When bishops teach formally or establish a binding discipline, the faithful owe obedience to them in their capacity as leaders who are responsible for the common good. Furthermore, Canon 753 mentions that, while bishops are not infallible, such as when the pope speaks *ex cathedra*, they are due the respect, gratitude, good will, and "religious submission" of the flocks they shepherd. Since they are fallible, their teaching is authoritative only when it's in harmony with the Magisterium of the Church.[10]

The Belgian Community's Special Secret

In the case of the 1859 apparitions of Our Lady of Good Help in Champion, the process of approval did not get underway in sincerity until 2008, when the bishop of the Diocese of Green Bay, Bishop David L. Ricken, launched an investigation into the matter. Up until that time, the apparition story and the chapel on the grounds had been part of pious tradition passed on from generation to generation. It was part of the DNA of the area. The local community, made up primarily of Belgian immigrants, accepted the apparitions as a matter of fact and saw no reason to pursue a formal investigation. They simply knew it as the Robinsonville Chapel (Robinsonville's name was later changed to Champion). Because of its quiet and somewhat remote rural location, the Belgian immigrants felt a sort of affectionate ownership of the site. All of Green Bay's bishops celebrated Mass there on special occasions, and some actively promoted the shrine. Still, it remained the special secret of the Belgian community. It was part of their heritage, and they were leery of the consequences should the place become widely known and frequented by strangers. They were not eager to lose the peaceful sacredness of the chapel and surrounding grounds. Additionally, there were concerns over the site's infrastructure, as it was not connected to a municipal water system, and the buildings themselves were not set up to accommodate large crowds of visitors.[11]

From the time of his 2008 installation as bishop of the Diocese of Green Bay, Bishop Ricken observed the happenings and development of the Champion shrine. Immediately, the question was put before him regarding what to do with the site and whether to grant approval of the apparitions. He wanted to learn more about it and get to know the people of his diocese before making any decisions. He knew that the site held a special place in the hearts of the locals, and he understood their protectiveness of it. He sympathized with their feelings and concerns and supported the activities at the shrine. But should he start the approval process? He took the matter deeply into prayer, waiting for a sign from God that would give him direction. It was an agonizing time for him.[12]

Eventually, the answer came in the form of a question: What is most needed today? To Bishop Ricken it was clear: evangelization and catechesis. In these two words lay the core of the message and mission Our Lady gave to Adele Brise during the apparitions. She instructed Adele to pray for the conversion of sinners and teach the children what they need to know for salvation. It was time to proceed with the approval process. Bishop Ricken asked three Marian experts to conduct a thorough investigation of Adele Brise and the apparitions at Champion. After a year of investigating, the experts arrived at their recommendations. Two were in favor of approving the apparition and one had a minor reservation. The reservation concerned the Belgian custom of holding a *kermis* — a social event that was similar to a parish picnic but often involved card-playing and alcoholic beverages — on the property during the celebration of the Assumption of Mary on August 15. This, however, was not in Adele Brise's control and did not impact the validity of the apparition itself. Taking the experts' findings into careful scrutiny, Bishop Ricken decided to approve the apparition of Our Lady of Good Help, an act he considers to be a great privilege.[13]

Formal Decree

On December 8, 2010, Bishop Ricken issued the following declaration granting formal Church approval to the apparitions of Our Lady of Good Help at Champion:[14]

CARITAS · SAPIENTIA · FORTITUDO

Most Reverend David Laurin Ricken, D.D., J.C.L.

By the Grace of God and the
Authority of the Apostolic See
Bishop of Green Bay
Decree on the Authenticity of the Apparitions of 1859
at the Shrine of Our Lady of Good
Help Diocese of Green Bay

GIVEN THAT

For over one hundred fifty-one years, a continuous flow of the faithful has come to Champion, Wisconsin, to pray, to seek solace and comfort in times of trouble and to petition Our Lord Jesus Christ through the powerful intercession to Our Lady of Good Help.

Incessant prayer has gone up in this place based upon the word of a young Belgian immigrant woman, Adele Brise, who in October 1859 said that the Blessed Mother, a Lady clothed in dazzling white, had appeared to her on this site.

The Lady was elevated slightly in a bright light and gave words of solace and comfort and a bold and challenging mission for the young immigrant woman. The Lady gave her a two-fold mission of prayer for the conversion of sinners and catechesis. "I am the Queen of Heaven who prays for the conversion of sinners, and I wish you to do the same. You received Holy Communion this morning and that is well. But you must do more. Make a general confession and offer Communion for the conversion of sinners. … Gather the children in this wild country and teach them what they should know for salvation. … Teach them their catechism, how to sign themselves with the sign of the Cross, and how to approach the sacraments; that is what I wish you to do. Go and fear nothing, I will help you."

Adele Brise began immediately to fulfill the mandate and mission entrusted to her by the Lady and oftentimes at great personal sacrifice went to the homes of the children to instruct them in the largely unsettled and forested area in Wisconsin. Adele was ever obedient to the authorities of the Church and steadfast in the mission entrusted to her by Our Lady, no matter what difficulty she encountered.

The mission given her became such a commitment that she set up a Catholic school of instruction for children and even began a community of Third Order Franciscan women, who assisted her in her obedience to the mandate of Our Lady to pray for the conversion of sinners and to instruct the children.

A long tradition of oral and some documented sources recounting answered prayers at the Shrine of Our Lady of Good Help include conversions and many physical healings attributed to the Blessed Mother's intercession. Many physical healings are memorialized by the multitude of crutches and other mementoes of thanksgiving for answered prayers left at the Shrine. Prayers for physical healing are answered even to this day through the intercession of Our Lady of Good Help. Though none of these favors have been officially declared a miracle by the Church, they are clear evidence of spiritual fruitfulness and the history of devotion to the Blessed Virgin Mary at the Shrine.

Graces have been poured out through the sacraments celebrated in this place especially through the celebration of the Mass and the Sacrament of Reconciliation, as well as through the recitation of public devotions and private prayers. Our Lady has lessened or relieved the burdens of the People of God, whether about financial, familial, relationship or employment matters or even through diminishing inclement and tempestuous weather.

This holy place was preserved from the infamous Peshtigo fire of 1871, when many of the faithful gathered here with Adele and prayed through the intercession of Our Lady of Good Help, with the result that the fire that devastated everything in its wake in this entire area stopped when it reached the parameters of the Shrine.

There is clear testimony to the upright character of Adele Brise, her devotion to Jesus Christ and the Blessed Virgin Mary, and her unwavering commitment to the mission Mary entrusted to her. Moreover, the uninterrupted history of faith and devotion testifies to the spiritual fruits bestowed upon the pilgrims to the Shrine.

GIVEN ALL OF THE ABOVE

Three Marian experts have studied the history of this alleged apparition and all of the extant documents, letters, and written testimonies in order to determine whether or not there are inherent contradictions or objections to the veracity of the testimony given by Adele Brise with regard to the events of 1859 and to establish whether or not there is enough evidence to suggest that the events which happened to Adele Brise may be of a supernatural origin.

The accounts of the apparitions and locutions are judged to be free from doctrinal error and consistent with the Catholic faith.

There is nothing in the person and character of Adele Brise that would question the veracity of the substance of her account. In fact, her personal character is a major factor in favor of the recognition of the apparition.

Objections concerning whether there was enough evidence to support a judgment in favor of the supernatural character of the events were thoroughly investigated and answered by the experts. The documents from the early history of the Shrine are not abundant, due primarily to the fact that Green Bay at the time of the apparition was frontier country. One of the experts affirmed that any lack of information does "not invalidate the overall impression of coherence between event and consequences, personality of the seer and commitment to the mission received, the comparability between this event and similar recognized apparitions, and challenges of the historical context and responses given.

GIVEN THAT

These simple apparitions and locutions given to Adele Brise became such a compelling theological and religious mission for her. The effects of these endeavors by her and many others have lasted these many years with such major spiritual benefit to so many people. Many of the local clergy and clergy from other Dioceses and Religious Institutes have come here on pilgrimage with their people, also with spiritual benefit.

All of my esteemed predecessor Bishops of the Diocese of Green Bay for the past one hundred and fifty-one years have been present for special Masses in Honor of Our Lady of Good Help, and some of them have even actively promoted the Shrine.

THEREFORE,

It remains to me now, the Twelfth Bishop of the Diocese of Green Bay and the lowliest of servants of Mary, to declare with most certainty and in accord with the norms of the Church:

that the events, apparitions, and locutions given to Adele Brise in October of 1859 do exhibit the substance of supernatural character, and I do hereby approve these apparitions as worthy of belief (although not obligatory) by the Christian faithful.

I encourage the faithful to frequent this holy place as a place of solace and answered prayer.

Given at the Shrine of Our Lady of Good Help, Champion, Wisconsin, the eighth day of December in the year of Our Lord two thousand and ten, the Solemnity of the Immaculate Conception of the Blessed Virgin Mary.

David L. Ricken

His Excellency, Most Reverend David L. Ricken, D.D., J.C.L.
Twelfth Bishop of Green Bay

Rev. John F. Doerfler
Chancellor

Chapter Two

BELGIAN EMIGRATION TO AMERICA

The southern end of Wisconsin's Door Peninsula is home to the largest settlement of Belgian immigrants in the United States, a settlement that began in the mid-1800s and spans five generations. Beginning at Green Bay and continuing to Sturgeon Bay, this tract of land contains a dozen contiguous townships inhabited almost exclusively by people of Belgian descent.[1] What brought them to this undeveloped and sometimes foreboding area along the shore of Lake Michigan? Why would they leave home, family, and friends to travel to this wilderness knowing they likely would never see their loved ones again? This is a fascinating story that tells us much about why the Blessed Virgin Mary appeared at Champion in 1859 to the young Belgian immigrant woman named Adele Brise.

God Paves the Way for the Belgian People

It seems God had destined Door County for the Belgian people when he sent Fr. Louis Hennepin to America in 1675. Father Hennepin, a Franciscan missionary from Ath in the province of Hainault, Belgium, played a prominent role in exploring the West. In 1679, Father Hennepin became one of the chaplains in Robert LaSalle's expedition to explore the Mississippi River. He was the first to describe Niagara Falls near the point at which LaSalle built his vessel, *The Griffon*. He sailed with LaSalle's party on the first vessel to sail the Great Lakes, braving these uncharted waters to reach Washington Island on the very tip of what would later become known as the Door Peninsula. Leaving the explorers behind, *The Griffon* embarked on its homeward journey but was never heard from again. All was lost, including a fortune in furs obtained from the Indians meant to defray the cost of the expedition.[2]

After *The Griffon's* departure, Father Hennepin and his group of about twenty men traveled by birchbark canoes to the southern end of Green Bay. The vicious autumn storm season inhibited their progress, and it took them a month to cover the approximately seventy miles' length of the peninsula. The group eventually made its way to the Illinois River, and from there Father Hennepin and two other men were sent to explore the upper Mississippi River. These were the first known white men to encounter St. Anthony Falls, named such by Father Hennepin himself, in what is now the center of Minneapolis, Minnesota. His return journey took him along the Wisconsin and Fox Rivers, with a short rest at the Jesuit mission on the site of what is now the city of DePere, Wisconsin, home of the National Shrine of Saint Joseph. At the end of his first day's journey, Father Hennepin found a suitable place to set up camp on the site of the present-day Village of Dyckesville, about twenty miles north of Green Bay along the peninsula's western shore. God's providence saw to it that this would later become the center of the largest Belgian settlement in America, covering an area twenty miles wide and fifty miles long.[3]

Life in Belgium in the 1800s

The next Belgian to come to the Door Peninsula would not arrive for another 174 years. In the Grez Doiceau commune of the province of Brabant, Belgium, a young farmer named Francois Petiniot made a business trip to Antwerp. During the trip, he stopped in a local tavern and found lying on one of the tables a brochure describing America. Such literature was a tool of the Immigration Official to recruit settlers from Europe to America. Particularly, Wisconsin solicited settlers for agriculture, promising them cheap land, freedom, and unlimited opportunity. The Official distributed thousands of pamphlets, posters, and booklets to Europe to entice emigration. For example, one poster read:

Come! In Wisconsin all men are free and equal before the law. Religion is free and equal between church and state. Opportunities are unlimited for those who want to work. Good land can be purchased from the generous American government for $1.25 an acre. The soil is adapted to raising corn, wheat, rye, oats, barley, and vegetables — all products with which the Belgian husbandman is familiar.[4]

The brochure Petiniot happened upon was written in Dutch, and Petiniot, having a basic command of the language, became intrigued by its content. The leaflet described America as a fertile land stretching for hundreds of miles. The land, it said, was vacant and prime for settlement. What's more, the $1.25 per acre was practically a pittance compared to the high cost of land in already overcrowded Belgium. Petiniot's farm in Belgium consisted of a mere four hektari[5] — hardly enough to adequately sustain his family. But in America, he could purchase a hundred times as much land for the same amount of money he'd receive for his land in Belgium![6] Petiniot kept the brochure and pondered the possibilities its contents might hold for himself and his family.

At the end of his business trip, Petiniot returned to his home enthused and filled with dreams of a better life in this new, promising country of America. After a few days of pondering, he shared his discovery and his enthusiasm with his family and neighbors. A few weeks later, neighbors gathered at this house to learn more and to discuss the feasibility of such a move. Petiniot pointed out the overcrowding in Belgium and the fact that their farms produced barely enough to sustain them. The best land belonged to lords who seemed unconcerned about the welfare of the poor who worked the lands for them. Even if there was land available, it would be priced far beyond their reach. He assured those present that America offered far more opportunity for their families, especially their children, who would grow up in a land of freedom and potential. Additionally, he told them, within a few years they'd become American citizens and have the right to vote.[7] Soon, the whole commune was buzzing with interest and talk of the amazing opportunity that awaited them across the ocean.

There were some, however, who doubted the authenticity of the brochure and the reliability of its information. They shook their heads, convinced that it was a scam to trick them into losing all that they had.[8] Going to America meant leaving family, friends, homes, churches, jobs, and the security of familiarity behind. Were they ready to do that for the sake of something hopeful, yet uncertain? These questions swirled in their heads and became the fodder of long and solemn family discussions. One might think of the Holy Family leaving all behind and heading to Egypt, a foreign land with foreign language, customs, resources, and without home or guaranteed source of income. Yet, Joseph, Mary, and Jesus went because they knew it was God's will for them. Was it God's will that the Belgians from the province of Brabant leave their homeland for a foreign country and an uncertain future? These were questions they had to ask themselves.

After some deliberation, Petiniot and nine other small farmers like himself decided to sell all that they owned and make the daring trip to America. The group consisted of Francois Petiniot, Jean Martin, Philip Hannon, Joseph Moreau, Etienne Detienne, Adrian Masy, Lambert Bodart, Joseph Jossart, Martin Pasque, and Jean Baptiste Detienne.[9] Some of these names have carried on through the generations and are still represented among Door Peninsula's current residents — a beautiful tribute to the courage and fortitude of the original Belgian immigrant families.

Because of the scarcity of land and abundance of population in Belgium, it didn't take long for the farmers to sell their properties. Taking the proceeds from their sales, they sought out the nearest agent who could help them secure passage on a ship to America. To their delight, they discovered that a three-masted schooner, *The Quennebec*, was scheduled to set sail from Antwerp to New York in the middle of May, and that there was room for them to travel aboard. The cost of a ticket for each person twelve years or older was $35, or about $1,036 in today's market.[10] In addition to the fee, travelers were expected to bring their own bedding and provisions for at least six weeks.[11] This required a scurry of activity, from gathering medical and personal care supplies, to baking and preserving food and beverages, and mending, sewing, organizing, and packing. There were legal tasks for the emigration process as well. Each traveler was required to have a birth certificate from his or her parish, an Emigration Permit from the local court, and a government passport.[12] Excited as they were, this must have been stressful on this small Belgian community of prospective seafarers. Once properly prepared, the group embarked on a one-week journey from Brabant to Antwerp where they would board the ship. At that time, such a journey across the ocean was considered a separation for life, and one can only imagine the tears shed during the final goodbyes to parents, aunts, uncles, siblings, and friends. At long last, *The Quennebec* set sail on May 18, 1853,[13] with the ten eager and anxious Belgian families and their luggage on board.

The Journey Begins

Once the journey began, the immigrants turned their attention to the journey itself and becoming acquainted with their fellow travelers. Perhaps it surprised them to see that copies of the same brochure that had attracted them to America had found their way into the hands of more than a hundred other emigrants from Belgium and Holland.[14] They, too, wished to seek their fortunes in the new land that promised a good life of plentiful land and prosperity. The voyage was a difficult one even for seasoned seafarers, but the Belgians, inexperienced at sea travel, found it that much more difficult. The trip included a succession of violent storms, and at one point, the ship's main mast snapped off and was carried away by the churning sea. By the grace of God, *The Quennebec* was able to carry on, swaying and creaking its way across the ocean for seven weeks. The final week brought heightened suffering for the emigrants as the passengers ran out of food and drinking water.[15]

In many ways, the arduous voyage across the Atlantic was nothing compared to the hardships the emigrants would face once they arrived in America. While on the ship, the Belgians decided to accompany the Hollanders to Wisconsin, as they had had no destination in mind when they left home. Using canal boats and lake steamers, they made their way through the Great Lakes waterways and eventually arrived in Milwaukee.[16] By comparison to their small home country of Belgium, the United States must have seemed unimaginably expansive, even though they had seen only a small portion of it! From Milwaukee, the Hollanders intended to go to Sheboygan, about fifty-six miles to the north along the Lake Michigan shore. They had friends there, and since the Belgians knew no one in this new and mysterious country, they decided to go along.[17]

Unfortunately, there was little land left in the Sheboygan area for them to settle upon. Additionally, they discovered that they could not communicate with the Sheboygan pioneers because they didn't know their language. The first settlers to that area were New England "Yankees" who spoke English. In the 1840s and 1850s, the region's demographic had changed and contained mostly immigrants from Germany, with some from Holland, Ireland, and other parts of Europe.[18] The Belgians didn't know any of these languages and found themselves surrounded by strangers on multiple levels.

Divine Intervention

By an act of Divine Providence, the Belgians eventually met a French Canadian. French being one of the most oft-spoken languages in Belgium, they were able to communicate adequately with the man. He told them that almost half of the population of Green Bay — an area just sixty-two miles farther north — spoke French. He also told them that in Green Bay the soil, timber, water, and climate were as good as those in the Sheboygan area. Encouraged, the weary travelers booked passage on a lake steamer and set off for Green Bay.[19]

There was indeed suitable land in Green Bay, and the men immediately made the thirty-five-mile trip to the government land office in Menasha to file land claims for each. They chose tracts in what is now the city of Kaukauna, about twenty miles southwest of the bay. Upon return to their wives and children in Green Bay, the men learned that the five-year-old son of Philip Hannon had succumbed to a previous illness and died the day before.[20] Obtaining their land had to be set aside for a few days as the Belgian settlers made funeral and burial arrangements. The loss of the child was a travesty, and yet God in his wisdom used this event as another stepping-stone on the path to the apparition of Our Lady in Champion.

Present at the funeral was the officiating priest's friend, Fr. Edward Daems. Father Daems, as you will see, was a key player in the happenings of the apparition. He was the pastor of Bay Settlement, then the last frontier settlement in northeastern Wisconsin and about ten miles north of Green Bay. Being also a Belgian, the young priest was friendly and enthusiastic about his mission of serving God's people in America. It would be a great help to his ministry, he told them, to have such faithful Catholics and fellow countrymen within his fold. He described the richness and beauty of the lands within his parish and explained that there were many French-speaking settlers there. With joyful persistence, Father Daems convinced Francois Petiniot and his companions to visit Bay Settlement to see for themselves the gifts that awaited them in what he had described as land of unsurpassed quality. He promised them that he personally would see to it that they procured pleasing sites on which to build their homesteads. What is more, they would be able to attend Mass, receive the sacraments, and participate in Divine Worship in their native language.

This sounded wonderful to the settlers, especially to the women. The group relinquished their claims in Kaukauna and followed Father Daems to Bay Settlement; he slowly drove his horse and buckboard while they traveled the winding dirt road through the forest on foot. Shortly after their arrival in Bay Settlement, they went with Father Daems and another guide to search for land on which to settle. They made their way through the already-settled areas and finally passed the last log cabin. They continued farther for many miles, finally deciding upon land ten miles northeast of Bay Settlement, and four miles south of Dykesville, in what came to be known as Robinsonville. As you will remember, Dykesville is the exact spot on which Belgian Father Hennepin had camped overnight in 1679. This landmark would play a role in the story of the apparitions of Mary to Adele Brise in 1859. The Belgians named their new settlement *Aux Premiers Belges*, or The First Belgians, and set about making America their new home.[21]

The young woman carefully made her way along the old Indian trail that led through the dense Wisconsin woods. It was a sunny October day, but you would never know it while walking through the forest because the trees blocked the sunshine. Occasionally she could see swatches of bright sunlight breaking through the branches high above her head, reminding her of the way God's love breaks through the darkness of the world and penetrates human hearts. On her head she carried a heavy sack of wheat her family had harvested on their homestead. Despite its weight, she managed it adeptly, as was the custom for Belgian pioneer women. With the narrow trails, the only way to the get the wheat to the grist mill was on foot, and she made her way swiftly along lest she encounter an unfriendly bear or wolf. One never knew in this wild country.

Just around the narrow curve in the path, Adele saw someone standing off to the side between two trees — a hemlock and a maple. It was a beautiful lady dressed all in white. Frightened, Adele stood still, wondering who this woman was and why she was there.

Although the woman looked Belgian, Adele knew she was not from Bay Settlement. From where, then? She had an unusual, almost mystical air about her that was both attractive and daunting at the same time.

As Adele gazed at the woman, the vision began to fade, until finally there was nothing left but a white cloud.

Chapter Three
THE METTLE OF THE BELGIAN PEOPLE

Wisconsin has long been lauded for the beauty of its glacial land formations and vast old-growth forests spanning acre upon acre of territory.[1] When the Belgian settlers arrived, the Door Peninsula was nearly covered with pristine primeval forests of cedar, pine, maple, hemlock, oak, and a variety of other coniferous and deciduous types of trees.[2] They chose for themselves a place deep in the ages-old forest where the tree cover was so thick sunlight could not filter through. This is where they would make their new homes, establish their farms, raise their families, and prosper. With grateful and hope-filled hearts, they set to work.

The First Winter
Their priority was to provide the basic necessities of life — food,

shelter, and clothing. Their first homes were three-sided huts with thatched roofs made from cedar and hemlock tree branches and just enough to protect them against inclement weather.[3] In this virtually untouched forest, they encountered more Native Americans[4] than people of European decent and were elated to find them to be friendly, welcoming, and helpful. Despite language differences, the Belgians and native tribes were able to communicate and establish a benevolent relationship.

The first winter was rugged, with terrible suffering. The Belgians were not accustomed to dealing with the harsh Wisconsin winters. The shelters they had constructed were inadequate to protect them from the bitter cold and drifting snow, with the howling wind making its way through the cracks and crevices between the branches. Without enough food, they faced the possibility of starvation in addition to the threat of freezing to death. However, the hardy Belgians faced the hardships with optimism, seeing them as a challenge rather than a blight. It was this spirit that allowed them to survive their first winter.[5]

Their optimism likely was aided by the friendship of the Native Americans. They taught the pioneers how to snare wild animals such as bear and deer, and smoke the meat to preserve it using traditional American Indian methods. In the spring, the Indians taught the pioneers their ancient art of tapping maple trees and, to their delight, making maple sugar.[6] Just as maple sugar had been an important part of the Native American diet, it would become an important part of theirs as well.[7]

Forging Homesteads

When the weather finally permitted, the Belgians began to clear their parcels of land. Without benefit of today's power saws, skidders, or stump grinders, they were able to clear enough land on which to build and farm — no easy feat given the thickness of the forest and size of the trees. The entire family helped with this strenuous and exhausting work. Since they already had plenty of firewood for themselves and there was no market for logs, they had to be rolled into a pile and burned.[8] They were able to find a few oxen, and with their help, they plowed the land between the large stumps left after the clearing and prepared for crop season.[9] Gradually, they were able to build log houses. They made doors by ripping logs into planks with a whip saw and using leather straps for the hinges. Mud was used to chink the openings between the logs and floors, and furniture was made of split logs. A box stove without an oven was used to heat the house, and handmade brick was used to build outdoor ovens that resembled a large fireplace. Bread could be baked in the outdoor ovens by heating the bricks to red-hot. In this way, more than a dozen loaves could be baked at a time. When the weather permitted, wheat, potatoes, and other vegetables were seeded in a clearing around the house to provide food for the family.[10]

On Sundays, they dressed in their best clothing and *sabots* — handmade wooden shoes — and walked ten miles one way to Bay Settlement for Mass. It was a gift for them to hear Father Daems celebrate Mass and give the homily in their native language.[11] Things were going well for the settlers. Life was good; they were content in their new surroundings, and confident about their future in America.

Letters from the New World

They were able to exchange letters with their loved ones in Belgium once a year, and in their letters home they boasted about the richness of their lives and described the beauty and bounty of their new home. These glowing reviews were proof — to their loved ones left behind as much as to themselves — that they had made the right decision in emigrating to this foreign land. Their happiness sparked the interest and stirred the hearts of family and friends back in Belgium, urging the naysayers to reconsider their original skepticism. Their letters described a life of abundance, in which the only thing necessary for becoming rich was two strong hands willing to work hard. Money and influence, they said, were unnecessary for success, and they spoke of a benevolent government that provided well for its people. The soil was rich and productive, and game for hunting was plentiful. The picture they painted was one of charm and opportunity.

Reading these impassioned reports, who would not be enticed to follow in the footsteps of the original Belgian emigrants? The settlers' letters were passed from one to another and eventually read by hundreds of Belgians back home. Emigrating to America — uncommon for Belgians at the time — was a new notion that struck them with awe and anticipation. Groups immediately began to depart for America, filled with joyful anticipation. By the fall of 1854, every log house in Aux Premiers Belges was cramped with new arrivals ready to seek their fortunes. The newcomers were welcomed with open arms in a current of jubilant reunions of families and friends after a long separation.[12]

The Cholera Epidemic

Sadly, their jubilation would soon turn into grief and terror. Along with news and greetings from back home, the new Belgian immigrants brought with them the deadly Asiatic cholera.[13] And so began a wave of deaths not only among the new immigrants, but also among those who hosted them. "Strong men, apparently well at night, would be found dead in the morning; the skin on their faces turned almost black and their eyes sunk far back in the sockets," wrote historian Hjalmar Rued Holand in his book, *Wisconsin's Belgian Community.* By this time, Father Daems's parish had grown to the point that it reached far into areas inaccessible by wagon. Because of this, the dead were buried in the back woods without coffins by a handful of close relatives. This left them without the Rite of Christian Burial or a priest to offer blessing and consolation to the survivors in their time of grief.[14] For this, Father Daems had to sternly admonish them. Since the Catholic Church professes belief in the resurrection of the dead and that the human body is an essential part of a person's identity, it requires that the bodies of the deceased be treated with respect and laid to rest in a consecrated place.[15] He told them that until they were provided with proper cemeteries of their own, several men must carry the dead in handmade coffins to Bay Settlement for Christian burial.[16]

Alarmingly, the news of the cholera epidemic traveled slowly and was not in time to warn the thousands of other Belgians preparing to emigrate. As the warning edged its way toward them, they were in the throes of frantic preparation. There was much to be done before they could depart for America. As sharecroppers living on the estates of wealthy landowners, they received little pay for their hard labor. With barely enough to live on day to day under normal circumstances, it took a long time to save up for passage on a ship and the supplies they would need along the way. Most of them were ready by the spring of 1856, and thousands of Belgian emigrants boarded ships to the new land and the prosperity for which they longed. Unfortunately, the journey was a disastrous one. It was an unusually stormy spring. One of the vessels was wrecked at sea, and all the several hundred Belgians on board, as well as the ship's crew, were lost. On another ship, the *David Otley*, there was an outbreak of dysentery, with sixty of the two hundred emigrants aboard dying. A third ship, the *Lacedemon*, became so storm-beaten and mangled that it drifted about on the sea for many days before it was finally able to return to Belgium. The delay forced the emigrants to use what cash they had for provisions as they awaited the next passage, and so they arrived in America penniless.[17]

By the grace of God, the weary travelers made it to Wisconsin at long last and claimed the majority of the vacant land on the Door Peninsula. Discouraged and impoverished, they faced a life of yet more hard work and scarcity. Some who were deeply disappointed wrote home to warn their relatives, but the letters did not reach them in time to deter one last wave of emigration in 1857.[18] Soon after, the mass emigration from Belgium to America dissipated. By 1863, more than 15,000 Belgians had emigrated to the Door Peninsula, the majority from the Brabant province.[19]

Scarcity and Financial Hardship

In due time, the money began to run out, making it necessary for the men to depart on foot for Green Bay, Milwaukee, and as far as Chicago, to find gainful employment. They were absent for weeks and sometimes months at a time, leaving the women and children behind to fend for themselves and stretch the already-scarce food and supplies yet further. The loneliness of those days remained long in the memories of the women who lived in fear of attack by hostile humans or wild beasts. Laughter and tears of rejoicing were heard from the log houses when the men returned with supplies and the bit of cash they could save while away. Sometimes their traveling packs contained gifts, too, like new kitchen utensils for their wives, colored hair ribbons for the girls, and candy sticks for the boys. With this new source of income, a time of prosperity followed, and the Belgian settlers were able to purchase farming implements and livestock to establish and increase their farms.[20]

In 1857, there was a severe economic depression in the United States that resulted in a widespread financial crisis. The crisis paralyzed most industries throughout the country, ending the employment of the Belgian men. The jobs they had held in places such as Green Bay, Milwaukee, and Chicago no longer existed, and they were left to their own devices for income. This forced them to look for ways to generate income within their own community and with their own resources.

Delight and Relief

They say that necessity is the mother of invention, and this proved to be the case for the struggling Belgians of Bay Settlement. They realized that they were surrounded by a major resource they had previously ignored — pine, hemlock, and other hardwood trees. When they first claimed their homesteads, they saw the trees as obstacles to building their farms. Now, they saw them as a source of income.

To their delight and relief, they discovered that pine logs were valuable and sold for $1.50 or more per thousand board foot. The only problem, however, was that they did not have oxen or horses to haul the logs out of the woods. Putting their heads together for a solution to this dilemma, they had the idea to make shingles out of the wood. Shingles would be far easier to transport, and they could sell them in Green Bay for $1.50 per thousand. So, they set about their new endeavor, felling the pine trees and cutting the logs into 18-inch bolts. These were split into half inch thickness with a tool called a froe,[21] and then the resulting shakes[22] were shaved into shingles with a draw knife.[23] Afterward, they were bound into bundles of fifty each. The bundles were carried to the bay shore and loaded onto a schooner from Green Bay. Without docks, the men transported the shingles on small boats and out to the schooner that was anchored farther out in the deep waters.

Soon every Belgian pioneer was engaged in this cottage industry, and up to four million shingles could be shipped in a single year. Eventually, they made enough money to purchase oxen or cows to haul the shingles to the shore and to plow the farm fields. The cows, of course, were also useful for providing milk for their families. And thus began another time of prosperity for the people of Bay Settlement.[24]

When the US Civil War broke out in 1861, it did not spare the Belgians of its grave consequences. By this time, they had become citizens, and the men were called into service for their country. Most were among the 91,000 Wisconsin men who served, more than 12,000 of whom lost their lives.[25] During the four years of conflict, fathers and sons were gone to war, and the women together with the men who were not called were left to work the farms as best they could. It was a common sight in those days to see Belgian women harvesting or plowing the fields with oxen, as well as doing other hard labor previously done by the men.

At the end of the war, the surviving men returned to Bay Settlement. Some returned to business and others concentrated on their farms. Sawmills began springing up in Bay Settlement, offering the men employment within their own community. Along with the sawmills came grist mills, providing the farmers with an efficient way to grind the grains they grew in their fields. Even after the devastation and death of the Civil War, the Belgian pioneers were able to resume the peaceful ebb and flow of rural life. This would continue for many more years.[26]

Chapter Four

BELGIAN FAITH
AND TRADITION

The Belgian people have their own specific character, and to merely classify them as "European" would be a great disservice to their exceptional heritage. It is this same exceptional heritage that gives us insight into the circumstances of the 1859 apparitions of Our Lady at Champion and the events that have followed from then until now. Who are these people in whose midst Our Lady appeared? Why did she choose them, and why at that specific point in history?

A Rich Heritage

The richness of the Bay Settlement heritage has been attested to by residents and researchers alike. Many of the customs which we will learn about here continue even until now. Historic facts and verbal histories form a charming mosaic of the colorful personality and tradition of this unique community who came to Wisconsin to escape the crop failures and industrial decline of their homeland in the mid-1800s. The Belgian immigrants of the Door Peninsula were Flemish Belgians who comprised one of the largest single groups of foreign settlers in Wisconsin and preserved more of the mother country's language, customs, and characteristics than other immigrant populations.[1]

The Belgians of Bay Settlement are Walloon Belgians who originally came from Wallonia, a French-speaking, Catholic region in Southern Belgium. Their language, customs, and heritage are distinct, and the legacy of their heritage is still observed across the region.[2] They form a compact community, and it is this same compactness that kept the Champion apparitions essentially a local secret for almost 150 years. Even now — five generations since the first group came to America — the last names of the first group of immigrants can be found in area directories, and some of these descendants still speak the ages-old Walloon dialect.[3] A 1987 study conducted by architectural researcher Dr. William Tishler showed that the area contains "perhaps the largest and most intact concentration of ethnic-related buildings surviving from any of the more than 30 nationalities who have settled in Wisconsin." In 1989, Namur — the community with the highest concentration of Belgian immigrants — was named a historic district and listed on the National Register of Historic Places by the US Department of the Interior. The following year, it was approved as a National Landmark.[4]

The Belgians of Bay Settlement have left their mark in industry and healthcare as well. From these early settlers sprang Joannes Brothers Company, a wholesale grocery business that later became Super Valu Inc. and is now associated with United Natural Foods, Inc. Dr. Julius Bellin, born of Belgian immigrant parents in 1870, founded what is now Bellin Health Systems by converting a small house in Green Bay into a clinic. Earl "Curly" Lambeau, whose grandfather came to Wisconsin from Belgium, became the founder of the Green Bay Packers. Fr. Bernard Pennings, a contemporary of Fr. Edward Daems, went on to found St. Norbert College and the Norbertine Order of Priests in De-Pere. The campus of St. Norbert College is home to the National Shrine of St. Joseph. These and many other such contributions to society are easily overlooked by those unfamiliar with the Belgian legacy that formed them.

Courage, Self-Reliance, and Laughter

The Belgians are a people of courage and self-reliance, as evidenced by their difficult sea journey and the way in which they conquered the nearly ninsurmountable challenges they faced in America. One account tells of the harsh conditions a group of weary immigrants encountered upon their arrival in 1856. Once they made it to Green Bay via a series of vessels and waterways, they disembarked with all their baggage at a primitive dock along the shore. From there, the settlers had to transport their belongings to Bay Settlement. They carried with them much more than the clothing, personal items, and sometimes food that accompany modern travelers. Among their things were supplies and tools for establishing their new life in a new land. As in one case, this could include a set of three-foot millstones for grinding grain into flour. Roads were few, and the ones that existed were crude and often unpassable in inclement weather. It was late November, a time when icy rain, snow, and freezing temperatures begin to envelope Wisconsin. The group had brought with them potatoes for sustenance, but also for planting. "It took the boat two days to deliver all our baggage. It was freezing quite hard and arriving at night they left all our stuff on the bay shore about three miles from our places with the result that all our potatoes were frozen," one account reads.[5] Loss of a primary food source is a crisis, yet even this did not crush their spirits.

Known for their jovial disposition, as one historian relates, the cliché, *crever ou etouffer de rire* — to split one's side open laughing — certainly pertains to the Belgian community. These are a sociable people with a festive spirit, eager to celebrate special occasions. Weddings, baptisms, family anniversaries, harvest time, and even being able to gather after Sunday Mass are causes of joy and community morale. It was natural for them, after Mass concluded, to cluster at the local pub to linger over a glass of beer while sharing the latest news and exchanging stories. This would also be an occasion to join in a game of *conion,* a card game and favorite Belgian pastime.[6]

The highlight of the year is the annual Walloon-Belgian Kermiss ("Churchmass"), a three-day harvest festival that takes place each September. The first Kermiss in America was held in 1858 in the village of Rosiere. It is an integral part of their heritage and is still celebrated today in both the Rosiere and Brussels townships. On alternating Sundays, a Mass of Thanksgiving is celebrated in the local church, followed by a procession with musicians, singing, and dancing. The procession makes its way down the street, pausing to dance at the crossroads. It culminates at a hall in which a large celebration is held, including more music, dancing, card-playing, and an array of Walloon beverages and delicacies — especially hundreds of Belgian pies. Belgian prune and apple pies are an exceptional treat, containing custard and topped with a thick layer of cottage cheese. Also among traditional foods are *trippe* (Belgian pork sausages), *kaset* (seasoned and cured cottage cheese spread), *jut* (cabbage and potato stew), and *booyah* (a thick chicken soup). Booyah dinners at church and community halls and parks remain a popular means of raising funds for charitable causes.[7]

Customs and Traditions

Walloon Belgian traditional processions come in other forms as well. The planting of the May pole takes place each May 1 at the conclusion of the election for town officials. An immense pole — usually made from a balsam tree and with a tuft of green at the top — is colorfully decorated with ribbons and streamers. The pole is planted at the front gate of the newly elected who stands in honor for the ceremony, after which follows hospitality and refreshments. There are several religious processions during the year. One example is the Rogation Procession, held in spring just before the feast of the Ascension. A crucifer leads the way, followed by little girls in white strewing flowers on the path, then comes the priest carrying the Blessed Sacrament. He is followed by the choir singing hymns and litanies. Behind the choir walk the women and finally the men. Musical by nature, the Belgians often participate in the processions with a diversity of instruments playing sacred music.[8]

The Walloon Belgians have a long history of religious devotion, and the vast majority are Catholic. They were serious about the practice of their faith, and so the scarcity of priests in the wild country of northeastern Wisconsin must have been a heavy cross for them to bear. One can understand that under such circumstances, attending a Sunday Mass was cause for deep joy, and religious celebrations and processions were never taken for granted. Initially, churches were great distances apart. It was not unusual for any one area to have a priest celebrate Sunday liturgy only once a month or even more rarely.

In the early years, the Walloons of Aux Premiers Belges had to walk ten miles in their *sabots* to Bay Settlement for Sunday Mass. From this reality sprang the development of roadside chapels, a custom that is unique to Belgian Catholics. The chapels, built by the families on whose property they stand, are typically nine feet long and seven feet wide and are used as a place of worship and to honor the Blessed Virgin Mary or another saint. Some have been built in commemoration of departed loved ones. A cross rests above the door or on the peak of the roof, and sometimes French inscriptions are found above the door. They have no windows other than the occasional window found in a door. The interior is painted in a pale color to draw attention to the altar that is placed directly opposite the door. On the altar can be found candles, flowers, small statues, and pictures of Our Lord, Our Lady, saints, or family members. These items always are carefully arranged in a symmetrical pattern, and a kneeler rests in front of the altar. It is customary to hang special documents such as birth, death, or marriage certificates on the walls giving witness to the family and as a symbolic welcome for visitors. A wooden chair offers a welcome spot to restfully meditate. Nearly every roadside chapel contains a guestbook, and guests are encouraged to sign their name and where they came from before they kneel or sit to pray. This structure was replicated throughout the Door Peninsula, and the chapels are situated close to the road as beacons for passersby. A significant number of them still exist and can be seen dotting the landscape across the peninsula. Today, travelers can follow a map that shows the locations of and routes to each of the chapels.[9]

Shrine historian and noted Catholic author Fr. Edward Looney is pastor to a cluster of Catholic parishes in the former Bay Settlement area. Born and raised just forty-six miles from there, he is familiar with both the region and the Belgian culture and has researched the roadside chapels, with the intenion of visiting each one possible. He gave his observation of this custom that speaks eloquently of the Belgian religious spirit:

During one of my trips to Belgium, I was dumbfounded when I discovered a roadside chapel in the middle of a road. The modern-day road was built around this chapel which I think emphasizes the importance of these chapels to Belgian heritage. They were places of devotion allowing people the opportunity to stop and pray as they passed by. In Wisconsin, the large number of Belgian immigrants brought this custom with them, erecting them often in gratitude for a grace received. In northeastern Wisconsin, some of the saints honored have a Belgian connection like St. Odile whose devotion was promoted by the Crosier Fathers or St. Ghislain. The chapels stand as a witness to faith, devotion, and heritage.[10]

It is impossible to adequately portray the Walloon Belgians in print. There is so much more to their character, culture, and heritage than can be written here. But perhaps this gives us some clue about what made them who they are. These are the people of Adele Brise, the people with whom she shares her roots. From this portrayal and information, we can begin to imagine what Adele might have been like and why the Blessed Virgin Mary may have chosen her to spread her urgent message and mission.

It was an eleven-mile trek from Adele's home to the nearest Catholic church. Despite the distance and difficulty, Adele would make the journey each Sunday, no matter how terrible the weather. For her, missing Sunday Mass was unthinkable! On this Sunday — October 9, 1859 — she was accompanied by her younger sister Isabel and a neighbor woman. On the way, the three women chit-chatted about the latest news from back home, the goings-on of the town, and the joys and sorrows of homesteading in America. They followed the same Indian trail as Adele had taken to the grist mill,

and as they approached the hemlock and maple trees, the same lady in white was waiting there for them. She appeared as before and in the exact same spot.

Adele was again frightened but tried not to let it show to her companions. Almost as if annoyed, she said, "O, there is that lady again." Her annoyance was minor compared to the overwhelming fear she felt. It made her unable to move. Her companions could see clearly that she was afraid but could not see the vision that appeared to her. Adele had told them what had happened the first time she saw the lady and shared her expectation that it was a poor soul in need of prayers. After a few minutes, the lady in white disappeared, leaving behind her a fading white cloud.

Chapter Five
FR. EDWARD DAEMS

A history of the apparitions of Our Lady at Champion would be incomplete without a chapter on the life and work of Fr. Edward Daems. Not only was he instrumental in bringing the Walloon Belgians to Bay Settlement, he also played an important part in the life of the Brise family and in the chronology of the Shrine of Our Lady of Good Help.

Father Daems was born to John and Catherine Daems on August 26, 1826. He was named Francis Edward, but always went by the name Edward. He had two siblings: a brother named John Hubert and a sister, Angelica. The Daems were a farm family and lived in the village of Schaffen, near Diest, Belgium. Sadly, Edward's father died when he was quite young, so he subsequently developed a deep attachment to his mother. Throughout his youth, Europe was in complete turmoil because of the Industrial Revolution, which upset family-centered livelihoods and instituted a factory system. What followed was a severe societal crisis, causing the less fortunate to suffer the most. In addition to the economic hardships, Catholics endured harassment and oppression by non-Catholics. In the meantime, the newly formed State of Wisconsin in the United States was putting forth its best efforts to lure dissatisfied Europeans to migrate and settle in the New World.[1]

Missionary Spirit

Father Daems was a member of the Crosier Fathers and Brothers, a missionary order that was founded in a small Belgian church by Blessed Theodore de Celle and his companions in 1210. The name Crosier comes from the French word *croisés*, which translated means "signed with the Cross." Hence, their primary feast day is the Exaltation of the Holy Cross (September 14 in the Roman Calendar). They are distinguished from other orders by the red and white crusaders' cross that is worn on the scapular of their religious habit. The order's charism is centered on a commitment to live and work harmoniously in community, to celebrate the prayer of the Church, to serve the people of God, and to welcome all with a spirit of hospitality. This includes a life of prayer and pastoral service inspired by the spirituality of the Holy Cross and based on the Rule of Saint Augustine.

From Belgium, the Crosiers spread their ministries throughout Europe and eventually internationally to the United States, the Democratic Republic of Congo, Brazil, and Indonesia.[2] The young Edward Daems was introduced to the Crosiers in 1845, when the order established a new foundation in Diest. A year later — at the age of nineteen — Edward Daems entered the novitiate of the Crosier Fathers and Brothers. The young novice was sent to Uden, Holland, to complete his studies for the priesthood and, in 1850, he was ordained. It was during this time that news of the hardships faced by the new American immigrants reached Europe. While the New World offered the promise of freedom and prosperity, it also placed overwhelming demands on them, taxing them physically, financially, and spiritually. There were few priests to serve them, and this attracted both the attention and concern of many religious orders back in Europe, among them the Crosiers. Reportedly, one immigrant wrote to his family in Holland, "If only the Crosier Fathers would know the dangers we are exposed to on all sides, they would come and help us."[3]

Off to America

The heart of the superior general of the Crosiers, Fr. Van den Wymelenberg, was touched by these pleas, and he wrote to Bishop John Martin Henni of the newly created Diocese of Milwaukee to obtain permission for the Crosier Fathers to come and work in Wisconsin. He also wanted assurance that his priests would receive shelter and subsistence when they arrived. Bishop Henni assured Father Wymelenberg that the Crosiers would be most welcome and cared for. In 1850, Father DeJonge and Father Nuyts were sent to Little Chute (not far from Bay Settlement) to assist Dominican Fr. Vanden Broek who was elderly and becoming mission weary. These priests were charged with establishing a Crosier foundation in the area. In September 1851, they were joined by Br. Peter Witvans and the newly ordained Fr. Edward Daems.[4]

Father Daems wrote of his first encounter with Fr. Vanden Broek:

> We were standing in front of some sort of dwelling which had been pointed out to us as the parish house in Little Chute. We had hardly recovered from the impression this ramshakled house had made upon us when a figure, more dilapidated than the dwelling itself, appeared in

the doorway. It was a man, spent by age, exhaustion, and sickness. He wore a red workman's blouse and a threadbare pair of trousers which were held up around his waist with a piece of rope. Two shoes of different design completed his non too clerical attire. Anyone else might have been scandalized by the appearance of a priest thus attired. Not me. I knew this man belongs to a rich family and had given everything away to the poor.

A new church was built in Little Chute and dedicated on the Feast of All Saints in 1851. Mass was celebrated by Fr. Vanden Broek, and at the end of his homily, he collapsed into the arms of Father Daems. He died two months later. Father Daems numbered among his greatest blessings the gift of knowing and being inspired by this holy, wise, and devoted missionary priest who had spent his life in the service of the Native Americans and pioneers of Wisconsin. [5]

Doctor, Social Worker, and Friend

The outbreak of Asiatic cholera devastated the immigrant community, providing Father Daems with ample opportunity to sharpen his skills as missionary, doctor, social worker, and friend to the sick and dying. The Crosier annals relate a story about a woman dying of the ravaging disease. Father Daems was called to her bedside late one evening and discovered that she had recently given birth to a baby boy. The poor mother was anxious about the child's welfare after her death, as there was no one else to care for him. After administering the Last Sacraments, Father Daems assured her, "Never mind the child, mother. I myself will take care of your boy." After the mother took her last breath, the gentle missionary priest wrapped the baby in his cloak and hurried back to the parish house. A message awaited him there informing him that another dying person needed his care, but this time at considerable distance away. Without a chance to notify Brother Peter about the little guest, Father Daems nestled the baby safely into his own bed and left to minister to the dying and their family. In the morning, Brother Peter was abruptly awakened by the piercing cries of a hungry baby. Thinking he was having a bad dream, the startled Brother tried to ignore the noise, but it continued. Upon discovering the baby, Brother Peter scooped him up and went in search of a neighbor woman, who tended the child until Father Daems's return. After his return, Father Daems entrusted the little orphan to a generous Catholic family who gave him a loving home, pledging to pay the expenses of his education. The story became public twenty years after Father Daems's death, affirming that his foster son had grown up to be a respected citizen and devout Catholic.[6]

In 1852, Father Daems was sent to Bay Settlement, at the time a desolate wilderness filled with dense forests and ancient Native American trails. Occasionally, one would encounter a crude log cabin burrowed in the woods. The unyielding challenges had forced all his predecessors into discouragement, exhaustion, and finally giving up. As the first resident clergy on the Door Peninsula, Father Daems poured himself into the demands made of him and the needs of his widespread parish. A small log church, known as Bay Settlement Church, had been built there in 1817, and upon his arrival he orchestrated the building of a new, much larger church, which he financed by begging for funds in both America and Holland and from his own family members. This same church served the area for the next eighty years, with Catholics from a ten-mile radius gathering there for Mass on holy days and Sundays.[7]

A Trusted Advisor

Father Daems was not only pastor to the Bay Settlement people, he was also a cherished friend and trusted advisor. There

were no roads, and so he traveled on foot to minister to his flock
— celebrating Mass, administering the sacraments in their log
cabins, baptizing their children, and burying their dead. Having
some medical training, he also served as their doctor, providing
remedies for their illnesses, and consoling the sick. His cheerful
and energetic demeanor made his visits a cause for great festivity
and rejoicing. Letters from home or other areas of Bay Settlement were few and far between, and there were no newspapers,
leaving the pioneers hungry for the latest news. Thus Father
Daems became a herald of sorts, sharing about the happenings
in his widespread parish (fifty miles long and ten miles wide —
a vast region to cover on foot or horseback with sparse, narrow,
rugged paths) and from what he knew of their homeland. Since
nearly all came from the same Belgian province of Brabant, they
looked forward to his news of weddings, funerals, and new arrivals from the old country. With his magnetic personality and
ready sense of humor, he told stories that were both informative
and highly entertaining. Father Daems was especially eager to
inform the settlers of the building of new churches in other areas
of the settlement, using this news as a powerful incentive for his
listeners to do the same. [8] Being able to speak Dutch, Belgian,
German, French, and eventually English made him an invalu-
able resource for the residents of the Door Peninsula.[9]

Transfers

Despite Father Daems's fruitfulness as pastor and popularity as
physician, adviser, and friend, his Crosier superiors in Holland
were sorely disappointed that a mission still had not been established by 1854. In fact, the Wisconsin Crosiers were unable to
live in community at all, being stationed a considerable distance
apart. Father Daems's faithful companion, Br. Peter Witvans,
had passed away and was buried in the cemetery in Little Chute
where Father DeJonge ministered. Father Nuyts had moved to

Manitowoc Rapids, and Father Daems was serving in Bay Settlement. Without experiencing the Wisconsin wilderness and its challenges himself, General Superior Van den Wymelenberg found it difficult to understand why a monastery had not yet been established.

The decision was finally made to found a monastery in Manitowoc Rapids with Father DeJonge and Father Nuyts working there. Father Daems was moved to fill Father DeJonge's vacant position in Little Chute. This saddened him, but he was resolute in following God's will and not his own. Shortly after his arrival in Little Chute, Father Daems was called back to Europe, as the need for him in Holland was greater. The exact date of his transfer is unknown, but it is certain that he was present in Belgium in time to teach at the College at Maaseik for the 1855–56 school year. In the meantime, a volley of letters was exchanged between the bishop of Milwaukee and the Crosier master general regarding Father Daems's exemplary work in Wisconsin. General Superior Van den Wymelenberg wrote to Bishop Henni:

> I gather from your letter that Confrere Daems is more able to be prudent in respect to founding a house of our Order than is Father DeJonge; for this reason, I am writing to return Father Daems to the mission of Little Chute, in spite of the inconvenience our Order will suffer because of his absence.

Still, the superior waited an entire year before acquiescing to the bishop's request. On September 21, 1856, General Superior Van den Wymelenberg wrote to Bishop Henni, informing him that Father Daems, accompanied by Fr. Anthony Aerts, Br. William Van Vlymen, and Br. Peter Huigens, would arrive in Wisconsin while Father DeJonge would return to Holland.[10]

Once returned, Father Daems immediately set to work on

the foundation of a Crosier monastery. Since during his absence Bishop Henni had promised Little Chute to the Marist Fathers, the Crosier community moved to Bay Settlement and began the construction of a new church. Yet again, Father Daems was called back to Holland, but not before he was able to complete the construction of the church. Bishop Henni dedicated the new Church of the Exaltation of the Holy Cross (later known as Holy Cross Church) on October 18, 1857. The old church building was used as the temporary home of the Crosier community until Father Daems was able to secure a tract of land from an elderly missionary named Father Bonduel. In compensation for the land, the Crosiers promised to pay Father Bonduel $200 a year until his death. He lived for four years, and after that the land became the property of the Crosiers. Unfortunately, Father Daems' monastery dream was interrupted again when he, as Superior of the American mission, was required to attend the order's 1859 General Chapter in Holland. During the Chapter, Father Daems was elected prior of the Crosier community near Diest, Belgium. He reluctantly accepted the position but resigned three days later. His heart remained with his Wisconsin mission territory and his people there. He returned to Bay Settlement in September of the same year.[11]

A Diminishing Community
Although the years 1852–57 had been prosperous for Wisconsin and its residents, it was not the same for the Crosier Community. The scope of their missionary work had become limited, no new novices arose from the local population, and none came from Europe. No one seems to know exactly what happened to the Crosier Community, but some speculate that members may have returned to Holland to avoid being conscripted into the military during the Civil War. In 1864, the *Catholic Almanac* no longer listed a Crosier monastery at Bay Settlement, and Father

Daems was alone at Holy Cross Parish. The only other two Crosiers left were Father Nuyts and Father Verhoff, who moved to a church in Potosi on the Mississippi where ill health and death eventually overtook them, ending the Crosier presence there. Father Daems's dream of a Crosier monastery in Wisconsin was not to come to fruition.[12]

As the population of the state grew, the main church at Bay Settlement was divided into fourteen smaller churches scattered throughout the Door Peninsula, and Father Daems immersed himself in serving them. The Holy See established the Diocese of Green Bay in 1868, installing Bishop Joseph Melcher as its first prelate. Soon thereafter, Bishop Melcher chose Father Daems as his Vicar General, signifying the level of respect the devout Crosier had earned in the diocese.[13] He held that position from June 1869 to May 1870 and again from the death of Bishop Melcher in 1873 until the installment of his successor, Most Rev. F. X. Krautbauer on July 2, 1875. His time as administrator was not without difficulty, as in those days the fledgling Catholic Church faced the challenges of pioneer times and a vein of trusteeism[14] that caused discord between pastor and parishioners and among the parishioners themselves.[15] Such discord would present significant problems for any temporary administrator, but Father Daems accepted them with grace and perseverance. He always had, and always would have, a loving pastor's heart.

A Common Education
Having been a teacher before he became a pastor, Father Daems was convinced that the surest way to unite his widely spread parishioners with their varying European cultures was to offer them a common education. From its inception, Father Daems took an active interest in the development of the Catholic school system in Wisconsin. He was confident that the catechizing and acclimating of the immigrants into American culture must be

tied to the diocesan structure. Acting on his inspirations, he built a parish school in 1865 — a primitive, one-room facility but nonetheless a functioning school. He staffed the school with religious sisters who understood the struggle of the immigrant peoples. In this manner, Father Daems was vitally instrumental in the establishment of Catholic schools on the Door Peninsula.[16]

Although he failed to establish the foundation for a Crosier monastery in the New World, Father Daems left his mark on the bedrock of the Catholic Church in northeastern Wisconsin, the history of the Door Peninsula, and in the hearts of the pioneers of Bay Settlement and their descendants. Clearly, Our Lady had chosen this holy missionary priest to participate in the message and mission she had for the Walloon Belgians and, through them, the entire United States and beyond. Historian Hjalmar Rued Holand said it best when he wrote in his book, *Wisconsin's Belgian Community*:

> The fate and fortunes of these many Belgians were largely affected by the guiding influence of Father Daems in persuading them to settle where they did. No doubt their early pioneers' struggles were made lighter by dwelling together in one large community with so many ties to bind them together. They have reason to feel grateful to his memory for he found them an excellent region to dwell in, and he spared no toil to help them.[17]

Chapter Six

ADELE BRISE AND HER FAMILY

In nearly all her apparitions, Mary has chosen to appear to simple, humble souls, yet has entrusted them with great missions. In Kibeho, Rwanda, she appeared to three unassuming high school girls, one of whom had only recently been baptized.[1] In Fátima, Portugal, she visited three shepherd children,[2] and in La Salette, France, she appeared to two shepherd children.[3] St. Bernadette Soubirous was a frail and uneducated fourteen-year-old peasant girl when Our Lady appeared to her in Lourdes, France.[4] None of these seers had high degrees of learning at the time of the apparitions, and all of them were of modest or poor means. It's also interesting to note that a large number of the people to whom Mary has appeared across the centuries were children or young adults. Perhaps she searched for childlike hearts that had not been burdened with the doubts and skepticisms so often found in the hearts of adults. Her maternal heart reached out to touch the hearts of children, knowing that they would take up her work without pretense, worldly interpretation, or ambition. Such was the case with the seer of Our Lady of Good Help.

A Promise to Mary

Adele Joseph Brise was born in Dion-le-Val, in the province of Brabant, Belgium, on January 30, 1831. Not much is known about her childhood except that she received minimal education and suffered the loss of one eye due to an accident with lye. As a child in Belgium, Adele attended a Catholic grade school run by the Ursuline Sisters. At the time of her First Communion, she, along with a small group of her friends, promised the Blessed Virgin Mary that they would join a religious order of missionary sisters and travel to foreign countries to teach the children.[5] This was not only her dream, but a promise that she took seriously throughout her life. As she was sure she was destined for the convent, the request from her parents to migrate to America meant the dissolution of her dream and abandonment of her promise to the Blessed Mother and to her friends. Not surprisingly, this caused an emotional and spiritual dilemma for her. In her reckoning, leaving her homeland would render her commitment impossible.

Troubled, Adele consulted with her parish priest about the heart-wrenching decision that lay before her. The wise priest told her that she should be obedient to her parents and honor their request. He assured her that, if God willed it, she would become a sister in America. Wanting to please God in all matters, Adele surrendered her dream and agreed to travel to the New World with her family. This likely brought Adele great sadness, and yet her trust in God was stronger than her sorrow and disappointment. At the time, her focus was on being a good daughter, and she had no idea that Our Lord had a crucial mission for her to fulfill in Wisconsin. In her new home, Adele joyfully poured herself into her new way of life and shared the struggles and burdens of pioneer life with her family and neighbors. Pioneer women worked endlessly in the care of the home and family as well as beside the men in the more strenuous labors. Like the other women, Adele worked in the fields, using primitive tools to prepare the soil for planting, carrying grain on their heads to the grist mill many miles away, and readying wood shingles for market in addition to the daily household chores.[6]

Emigration to America

On June 9, 1855, Lambert and Marie Catherine Brise left Belgium with their three children: Esperance, twenty-seven; Adele, twenty-four; and Isabel, twenty. They were accompanied by Adele's second cousin, Vital, age five. After a mild seven-week voyage, the family landed in New York. Without delay, they headed westward to Wisconsin where they quickly established a homestead. Records show that on August 7, 1855, Lambert and Marie bought 240 acres of farmland in Red River for $125.[7] Historical accounts relate stories of Lambert Brise's ten to twelve years of involvement in the founding and development of the National Shrine of Our Lady of Good Help, but there are no accounts of what happened to Lambert, Marie, or Adele's siblings beyond that point in time. Whether relatives of the Brise family also immigrated to America is unclear. However, land claim records show that on June 27, 1859, a man named Octavius J. B. Brice (Brise) filed a claim for ninety-seven acres of land in the Town of Union on the Door Peninsula.[8] Additionally, historical accounts and documents list two possible spellings for the family's last name: Brice and Brise. It was later determined that Brise would be considered the conventional spelling.[9]

Adele's Piety and Simple Ways

From a young age, Adele had an innate religious disposition and was known for her piety, simple religious ways, and love for nature. In one of the first devotionals dedicated to her after her death, the author described her this way:

> She shrank from vain pleasures that entice the heart of the young, for she always carried her mind towards God and his service. ... In the quietude and silence of a place where the noise of the world had not yet found its way, surrounded by the mystic murmur of the woods, her mind grew serious. Her thoughts turned more and more towards the supernatural, and life had for her the sole purpose of serving God with love and faithfulness. All that [knew her personally] could at once perceive the beauty of this simple soul, wherein the grace of God loved to dwell. Simple and sincere in her ways when a child, she remained thus all her life and this must be the cause why her personality attracted everybody.[10]

Many years later, a priest familiar with Adele and the trials she faced said of her:

> Adele was poor in point of fortune and physical attractions but rich in grace and virtue. ... Those who knew her during her childhood in Belgium assured me she had always distinguished herself by her fervent piety, ardent love of her neighbor, and unbounded confidence in the Blessed Virgin. Today, all those who have any [dealings] with her perceive at once that time has only developed and strengthened more fully these virtues in her heart.[11]

It is no wonder, then, that Our Lady chose to appear to this young Belgian immigrant woman and entrust her with the responsibility of carrying out her divine mission to teach and spread the Catholic Faith. She needed someone with an unassuming temperament, a strong constitution, and a God-loving heart, and she found that in Adele Brise.

Chapter Seven
THE APPARITIONS

The young Adele Brise seemed to have acclimated well to her new life in the forests of northeast Wisconsin. The first four years were relatively uneventful, and her life took on the pattern of most immigrant families — hard work, frugal living, and simple joys. Adele's faith remained vital to her, and she looked forward to receiving the sacraments despite the eleven-mile walk (one way) to her parish church in Bay Settlement — the nearest and only Catholic church in the area at the time. Like other pioneer women, she carried heavy sacks of wheat on her head to the grist mill several miles away so that it could be ground into flour for baking the family's bread.

The First Apparition
It was on one of Adele's trips to the grist mill[1] that the first of three apparitions took place. An account was written years later

by Sr. Pauline LaPlante. As a close companion and collaborator in Adele's mission, Sister Pauline often heard what happened directly from Adele's lips.

In early October 1859,[2] Adele was following an old Indian trail that led through the wilderness toward Dykesville and later branched off to Bay Settlement. She was carrying a sack of wheat on her head to the gristmill when she suddenly saw a lady all in white standing between two trees — a maple and a hemlock. Adele was frightened and stood still, not knowing what to make of it. The vision slowly disappeared, leaving a white cloud behind. Once the vision had faded, Adele continued on her errand and returned home without seeing anything more. When she got home, she told her parents what had happened, and they wondered what it could be. They thought perhaps it was a poor soul who needed prayers.

The Second Apparition

The second apparition of the beautiful lady took place as mysteriously and briefly as the first. The following is an excerpt from the National Shrine of Our Lady of Good Help History:

> On the following Sunday (October 9) she had passed here again on her way to Mass at Bay Settlement, which was the nearest place, about 11 miles from her home. Despite the great distance and the inclemency of the weather, Adele would never miss Mass on Sunday. This time she was not alone but was accompanied by her sister Isabel and a neighbor woman. When they came near the trees, the same lady in white was at the place where Adele had seen her before. Adele was again frightened and said almost in a tone of reproach, "O, there is that lady again."
>
> Adele had not the courage to go on. The other two

did not see anything, but they could tell by Adele's look that she was afraid. They thought, too, that it might be a poor soul that needed prayers. They waited a few minutes and Adele told them that it was gone. It had disappeared as the first time, and all she could see was a little mist or white cloud. After Mass Adele went to confession and told her confessor how she had been frightened at the site of a lady in white. He bade her not to fear and to speak to him of this outside of the confessional. Father Verhoeff[3] told her that if it were a heavenly messenger, she would see it again and it would not harm her, but to ask in God's name who it was and what it desired of her. After that Adele had more courage. She started home with her two companions, and a man who was clearing land for the Holy Cross Fathers at Bay Settlement accompanied them.[4]

The Third Apparition

Adele kept in mind the instructions Father Verhoeff had given her in case the mysterious Lady appeared to her again.

As they approached the hallowed spot, Adele could see the beautiful lady, clothed in dazzling white, with a yellow sash around her waist. Her dress fell to her feet in graceful folds. She had a crown of stars around her head, and her long golden wavy hair fell loosely over her shoulders; such a heavenly light shone around her that Adele could hardly look at her sweet face. Overcome by this heavenly light and the beauty of her amiable visitor, Adele fell on her knees.

"In God's name, who are you, and what do you want of me?" asked Adele as directed.

"I am the Queen of Heaven who prays for the conversion of sinners, and I wish you to do the same. You received Holy Communion this morning and that is well. But you must do more. Make a general confession and offer Communion for the conversion of sinners. If they do not convert and do penance, my Son will be obliged to punish them."

"Adele, who is it?" said one of the women. "O, why can't we see her as you do?" said another weeping.

"Kneel," said Adele. "The Lady says she is the Queen of Heaven."

Our Blessed Lady turned, looked kindly at them and said, "Blessed are they that believe without seeing."

"What are you doing here in idleness," continued our Lady, "while your companions are working in the vineyard of my Son?"

"What more can I do, dear Lady?" said Adele weeping.

"Gather the children in this wild country and teach them what they should know for salvation."

"But how shall I teach them who know so little myself?" replied Adele.

"Teach them," replied the radiant visitor, "their catechism, how to sign themselves with the Sign of the Cross, and how to approach the sacraments; that is what I wish you to do. Go and fear nothing. I will help you."[5]

Surrounded by a luminous atmosphere, the Blessed Mother raised her hands as though giving her blessing to those kneeling at her feet. Then, slowly, she vanished from sight, leaving Adele overwhelmed and prostrate on the ground, and the dense woods as solemn and silent as before.

News of the Apparitions Spreads

The pioneers living in the area were astonished when they heard what had happened to Adele. Most of them believed Adele's story, but there were some who thought Adele had psychological problems and may have manufactured the entire narrative. Her family did not doubt her story, and her father, Lambert Brise, built a log chapel ten-by-twelve feet near the place of the apparitions. Inside was an image of the Immaculate Heart of Mary, given to Adele by her confessor, Father Verhoeff, a fellow Crosier of Fr. Edward Daems.

Sister Pauline had vivid memories of having visited the chapel as a child. "I knelt in the clear little chapel and sang with Adele her favorite hymn in French, *Chantons le Nom Admirable de la Reine des Cieux* ('Sing the Wonderful Name of the Queen of Heaven'). After the death of my mother in 1863, I visited Adele oftener, but it was always a pleasure to look back to my first visit to the dear little chapel."

She also recalled Adele's sadness at some of the words spoken by the Queen of Heaven:

> She often told us how grieved she was to leave Belgium because she intended to join a religious community where she had made her First Communion. She and several of her companions had promised Our Lady at that time to become religious and devote their lives to the foreign missions. The other girls followed their vocation. That was why Adele felt so sorry when Our Blessed Mother said to her, "What are you doing here in idleness while your companions are working in the vineyard of my Son."

Sister Pauline went on, "So many times we would gather around Adele and have her tell us of the apparitions of Our Blessed

Mother. She would always tell us in the selfsame way how she saw her twice without Our Lady saying a word, but at the third time she spoke to her, she gave her the message of instructing the children in their religion, lest they should lose their faith."

No Opportunity Wasted

Adele never wasted an opportunity to mention the apparitions to others, and was eager to confirm details or answer questions about the miraculous events. This is exemplified in the letter below:

Dear Friends,

I received your letter and it fine (*sic*) us all well thank God and his Blessed Mother, hoping that these few lines will find you all the same. And please tell Mr. Papineau that his little boy is well & happy thank God and he send (*sic*) his love to his Papa and Brothers. Your little girl and also Mr. Poirier's little children are well & good little children.

Dear Friend you asked me how long since the Apparition of the Blessed Virgin. It was 30 years the 9th of last Oct. of what she appeared for the last time. It was the day she spoke and said to pray for the conversion of the Sinners & to instruct the little children in their religion & for the rest you must excuse me I have no time to discrip (*sic*) you more for I have to (*sic*) much to do but you may be sure that we will pray for your Uncle in the Chapel at the foot of the Alter (*sic*) of our good Mother.

Dear Friends I will send you a Medal for your Uncle that is sick, hoping that he is well now if it is the will of God.

All the Srs. send you their best respects. From your trauly (*sic*) friend

Sister Adele

These are Adele Brise's words in a letter dated November 25, 1889, and addressed to Mr. and Mrs. J. Demers of Marinette, Wisconsin. As was her custom, Adele dictated all her correspondence to her secretary, and this one was no different.[6] In the letter, she mentions children in her care, other "Sisters," and "the Chapel." These refer to a chapel built upon the apparition spot, the children's boarding school she eventually established, and the tertiary community she founded. We will go into greater detail about those things in coming chapters. The letter is included here because it offers us insight into the impression Mary's visit made on the heart of this Belgian immigrant woman when she was twenty-eight years old. Adele's words clearly reflect her clarity of mission and strict compliance to the instructions given her in the final apparition. She did not have time to dictate more than a few lines to her friends because she labored tirelessly and joyfully night and day. Her primary occupation was completing the work entrusted to her by the Blessed Virgin Mary.

While the faithful are not bound to believe in apparitions, they are an important facet of our Catholic faith and a means by which our faith may deepen and our understanding of the divine grow. The *Catechism of the Catholic Church* explains it this way:

> Throughout the ages, there have been so-called "private" revelations, some of which have been recognized by the authority of the Church. They do not belong, however, to the deposit of faith. It is not their role to improve or complete Christ's definitive Revelation, but to help live more fully by it in a certain period of history. Guided by the magisterium of the Church, the *sensus fidelium*[7] knows how to discern and welcome in these revelations whatever constitutes an authentic call of Christ or his saints to the Church. (67)

The number of people who could testify to the faith, piety, and integrity of Adele's character give credibility to her visions of the Blessed Virgin Mary.

Adele's life was forever changed by the visit of the Queen of Heaven, and she never doubted her intercessory power or the providence of God. Her profound trust and certainty of the apparitions would be the guiding light that illumined the path of the mission given to her by Our Lady on that chilly October 9, 1859, in the wild woods of northeastern Wisconsin.

Chapter Eight

ADELE'S MISSIONARY ZEAL

Adele's response to Our Lady at the apparition was not un-like the Blessed Virgin's response to the angel Gabriel at the Annunciation. Upon receiving Mary's instructions to "gather the children in this wild country and teach them what they should know for salvation," Adele had one question: "But how shall I teach them who know so little myself?" Her question was not whether she would undertake the mission that was asked of her, nor what reward she would receive in return. Rather, she questioned her own adequacy to carry out the demanding mission set before her, given her lack of education.

Upon receiving God's instructions from the angel Gabriel, "And behold, you will conceive in your womb and bear a son, and you shall call his name him Jesus" (Lk 1:31), Mary had one question: "How can this be, since I am a virgin?" (Lk 1:34, NRSVCE). She did not question whether she wanted to follow God's will or what she might gain in return for consenting to his request. Rather, she questioned how it could be that she would conceive a child when she had taken a solemn vow of virginity and remained a virgin. The responses of both women demonstrate a pronounced spirit of humility and desire to please God. For both women, the dilemma was not in following God's will but in being worthy and equipped to carry out the mission entrusted to them. Likely the similarity was borne of a deep, mutual love between the Blessed Virgin Mary and Adele Brise.

Wild Country and Its Challenges

Our Lady's commission to teach the Catholic Faith to the children in "this wild country" reflected the spiritual dangers they faced. The times were dire for Catholicism in America. In nineteenth-century Wisconsin, ethnicity was a critical element in the social fabric of the immigrants. Typically, cultural heritage determined one's religion and politics, in addition to the daily aspects of life such as way of dress, types of foods, trades and skills, and other customs. Wisconsin became a prime location for hundreds of thousands of immigrants because it offered an abundance of inexpensive land, industrial jobs, and a free political climate. For these settlers, ethnicity was a key factor in choosing a place to live, since immigrants tended to cluster together in their ethnic communities named for locations in the old country. These communities became their "home away from home," as it were, and offered the comfort of familiar languages and customs that made them feel at home amid the dominant Yankee culture.[1] As the settlers did not have a common language at the time, language barriers prevented many local churches from fully addressing the pastoral needs of the people. If they could not understand the liturgy, how could they participate in it? Eventually ethnic-specific churches were created to meet this challenge but not in time to stop the spread of apathy among the settlers in practicing their Catholic Faith.[2]

The problem was compounded by the fact that churches were few and far between, and there were even fewer priests to minister to immigrant Catholics. In a letter dated July 5, 1855, Rev. John C. Perrodin, then pastor of St. John's Catholic Church in Green Bay, wrote to his confrere Rev. M. Charles à Gottechain in Brabant, Belgium, describing the plight of the Catholics in northeastern Wisconsin and the dilemma he faced in serving them:

> For the spiritual account unfortunately, there is much to lose for the Catholic immigrant; those who have the faith make an effort to buy land near a church, but alas, how many are there through poverty and often through indifference settle far from church. They end up by neglecting their duties of religion and live as unbelievers. The children are not instructed and grow up without knowing God. …
>
> I hope the Belgians will have a church, cemetery, and a Catholic school, but alas who will officiate for them. I am the only Catholic priest in three counties, yet I have 2,000 Catholics in this vast territory.[3]

Religious Devotion Wanes

No doubt this influenced the religious practice — or lack thereof — of the settlers. Already they faced great hardship, and their waning faith made life that much more difficult. Worse, lurking among them were self-declared preachers who threatened to lure Catholics further from their faith by teaching heresy. The impassioned priest spared nothing to fight for the souls of the people he loved and pastored. An 1856 letter to the editor of the

Green Bay Advocate written by Father Perrodin describes one such threat and his stern rebuttal of the perpetrator:

> Mr. Editor: – The circular of a certain Mr. Schnitzler which I have read in the last number of the Advocate, contains assertions which is my duty to correct. I, therefore, respectfully request you to publish the following:
>
> Caution to the Public! Beware of false prophets. When the devil tempted Christ, he quoted the Scriptures, and God permitted it to guard his servants against a more hypocritical display of scriptural quotations. By their fruits you shall know them. Now Mr. Schnitzler you state that you will devote your labors, especially to the two thousand Belgians in our midst who are without evangelical instructions and preaching, and who, as a German settler, have chosen you by subscription as their preacher. This I must call an untruth. Two thousand Belgians have chosen you! Indeed, can you produce the names of two hundred, nay, of twenty? Have you forgotten your text, that liars shall have their part in the lake which burns with fire and brimstone? When a man carries lies and calumnies in his basket or his buggy, I may forgive him on the ground that he is an idiot; when a man willfully and knowingly states as facts, what he knows to be false, he must be marked as an impostor. The great majority of Belgians are Catholics. Can you deny it? Besides, the Christians who are despised (chiefly through the tracts which you spread through the land) and persecuted by all sects and by the "Know-Nothings" are members of the Catholic Church. Can you deny it?
>
> These few lines I send you as my New Year gift to moderate your zeal.

Truth in love is a fine motto, but love of truth is the best of all.
JOHN PERRODIN
The true pastor of the Belgians in Brown County.

Delving into Her Mission

After having received her commission of catechesis and evangelization from the Queen of Heaven, Adele wasted no time delving into the mission that would become her lifelong vocation. She was a simple lay woman, uneducated but pious, who saw herself as unfit for such a momentous task. Yet despite her simplicity and meager education, she was wise in the ways of the Lord. The Blessed Mother understood Adele's hesitations and self-perceived shortcomings, and so she provided precise instructions that were drawn from Adele's own formation in the Faith. She did not require Adele to obtain further education, but rather that she teach from what she already knew — her abiding love of God and the Blessed Mother. In this way she fulfilled the divine plan for her life.

According to Fr. Edward Looney:

Adele could not leave her experience along that Indian Trail — it became a part of her being. Going forth from the apparition mystified, and having been sent as a missionary, Adele returned home to share her encounter and message with her parents, sisters, and everyone she met. Immediately following the apparition, Adele devoted her life selflessly to the cause of catechesis.[4]

Adele accepted her duty with joy and determination, even though it meant arduous labor and heavy burdens. She assumed the role entrusted to her with the armor of her faith and confidence in Mary's promise of help. Unflagging in her commitment, she set out in search of children to whom she could teach the Faith. For seven years, she traveled up and down the Door Peninsula, traversing a radius of fifty miles in every type of weather, including the scorching summer heat, bitter winter temperatures and mountainous snowfalls, and the cold wind and rain of Wisconsin springs.

Facing Risks and Adversity

She faced other risks as well. Recall that at this time there was little, if any, wheeled traffic, and the only road was the Indian trail shared by bears (including protective mother bears accompanied by their cubs), herding deer, prowling timber wolves, and perhaps an occasional hungry bobcat. As if that were not enough adversity, Adele faced extreme fatigue and abundant ridicule from naysayers. Undaunted, she would walk from village to village and home to home across great distances, knocking on doors and offering to do housework and other chores for the families in exchange for permission to catechize the children. In her encounters, she also gently admonished the sinner, always encouraging others to live their faith with fervor and follow God's commandments. Once she considered the children to be sufficiently prepared, she brought them to the pastor at Bay Settlement for examination. After his examination, he admitted them to their first holy Communion.

Sister Pauline, one of Adele's early collaborators, recalled, "I remember well as a child, she would come with her little band of children to Bay Settlement, kneel at the foot of our Lady's altar and sing hymns with them in French. Adele had a sweet voice and possessed a charm that drew the young to her. I would kneel behind her with a burning desire to follow her."[5]

An observer for the *Kewaunee Enterprise* wrote of her:

With patience and earnestness that never flagged, she

persevered in her mission going from house to house, and helping unsolicited to do whatever work there was to be done in the household — asking only in return that she be permitted to give instruction to the children. Her great piety, her disinterested zeal, her kind and sympathetic nature and her blameless life soon won for her a respect among the people with whom she labored that was almost reverence.[6]

The severity of the adversities she faced despite her own weaknesses and shortcomings give witness to the fact that the apparitions could not have been a mere figment of her mind. Who would withstand such hardship if it were not a divine calling? The fruitfulness of her holy endeavors gave further testimony that this could only be a work of God.

Dawn of the Pilgrimage Movement

As Adele's ministry spread, so did the story of the apparitions. Pilgrims arrived in large numbers almost daily to visit the apparition site and the small log chapel built by Adele's father. Before long, the tiny structure became too small to accommodate all the visitors. In 1861, Lambert Brise, with the help of other settlers, built a larger chapel, this one twenty-four by forty feet.

An impressive account was given by a writer for the *Kewaunee Enterprise* regarding his interview with Adele. He wrote:

She conducted us first through the chapel — a small church edifice capable of sitting about one hundred persons, and over the entrance on the exterior was written the inscription, '*Notre Dame de bon Secours, priez pour nous*' ['Our Lady of Good Help, pray for us'].

In the auditorium, low painted benches without backs answered the purpose of pews, but the sanctuary and the

altar were richly and expensively decorated with paint-
ings, images, and silverplated. On one of the side walls of
the chapel were hung eight crutches, said to have been left
by cripples who had been cured of their lameness through
the instrumentality of Our Lady and which are regarded
as ever present witnesses of her power.[7]

A New Community Emerges

Over the years, the number of children increased while Adele's
energy began to decrease. Years of trudging through the wilderness in inclement weather and pouring herself out in the service
of the children had worn her out. In 1865, the Belgian colony
received a new pastor, Rev. Phillip Crud. Father Crud was so impressed with Adele's sincerity, and with the success of her work,
that he advised her to form a community of women who would
share her mission, thus lightening the burden she had carried
alone for so long. He was sure that Our Lady wanted the work
to prosper.

Adele took the priest's advice, and by 1864 she had gathered
a group of three like-minded women, founding with them a lay
community of women who lived together in a farmhouse not
far from the chapel. Adele did not seek canonical approval for
her newly founded community to become a formal religious order. Instead, the group of women became Third Order Secular
Franciscan — non-vowed laywomen who chose to live together
following the Franciscan way of life. Because they took no formal vows, the women were free to leave whenever they wished,
but their conviction of the mission and loyalty to Adele bound
them together. Even though they were not a religious order, they
were still addressed by the settlers as "Sister" and wore a modi-
fied habit like that worn by Franciscan religious. They became
known as the Sisters of Good Help, named after the inscription
above the door of the 1861 chapel.[8] However, Adele referred to

them as the Sisters of St. Francis of Assisi.[9] Before long, they were joined by two other women willing to serve the Queen of Heaven in Robinsonville.

Building a Convent and School

Additionally, Father Crud urged Adele to appeal for funding to build a convent and school. This way the children could come to Adele for instruction, and at the same time she would be able to conserve her own health and strength. He supplied her with a letter of recommendation, and with that and accompanied by an English-speaking companion, she began the first of many begging tours throughout the area. In her book *Patron Saints*, Eliza Allen Starr wrote about being visited by Adele during one of her fund appeals:

> On one of the warmest days of this last summer, coming into my little parlor, I saw two women seated there, dressed in black serge gowns and cloaks, and wearing bonnets exactly like the cape-bonnets that little girls still wear. Theirs were made of black berège with narrow strips of pasteboard run in, to make them stand out from the face. It gave an air of rustic humility to their costume. I welcomed them as "Sisters" of some order unknown to me, and found that only the youngest could speak English; but a letter in choice French from Rev. Father P------- of Robinsonville, near Green Bay in Wisconsin, gave me a clue to the mystery before me. It introduced me to Sister Adele, a humble Belgian woman, to whom had been granted undoubtedly, an apparition of our Blessed Lady, leaving her to tell me, through her young interpreter, the story of her graces and of her labors. …
>
> Sister Adele had no "price" for teaching, no tuition

bills to make out to her pupils even at the end of a whole year; and their parents, finding the school a free school, were glad to send their children. Once started, there was no lack of scholars; and very soon, Adele found her room was too small for her school. Then this courageous woman undertook to beg, from more favored communities, the money necessary for building a large schoolhouse, then a Chapel, and, finally to raise a home for the religious, whom she hoped to persuade to assist her in her great work. It was on this errand that she had come to our city, where churches and schools, and sisterhoods flourish, and there were few hearts on which her appeal fell unheeded. … Sister Adele does not yet belong to any religious Order, but if she ever does, I hope she will wear her simple cape-bonnet, as a memorial of the rustic garb in which she met the Queen of angels and of saints, and received her commission to teach the little ones of the "household of faith."[10]

In 1864, a frame residence and school were built on the chapel grounds.[11]

Begging Tours and Pleading Mary's Help

Despite the success of her fundraising appeals and her resolve to make charity a keynote of her work, Adele discovered that the institution she had founded could not subsist on contributions alone. She needed income to continue her mission. Countless old settlers told how their fathers would take their teams and accompany Adele on begging tours through the countryside, asking the farmers for vegetables, grain, and meat so that she could feed her Sisters and the children who now lived on the property as boarders as well as students. Even with the generosity of the farmers, it was not uncommon for the community to lack provisions. As one of the Sisters remarked, "Often we did not know what we would have for breakfast." Whenever that happened, Sister Adele would gather her companions after the children were in bed and go to the chapel to pray and beg for Mary's help. Without fail, they would find a bag of flour or a supply of meat left at their door by morning. Many of the children brought supplies from home as a way of compensation for room and board and education. But even that did not always keep the wolves from the door.[12] However meager their rations and supplies, it is remarkable to note that Sister Adele always assured that the children felt well cared for and loved.

The exact date is not known, but records show that the new school was in operation sometime between 1867 and 1868. In 1869, the school formally opened as St. Mary's Academy.[13] Regarding the new school, an article in the county paper stated the following:

> When therefore she conceived the idea of founding a Convent and school to enable her the better to achieve the object for which she labored, she experienced little difficulty in obtaining the necessary means, and about four years ago, the Convent of the Sisters of Good Health[14] was established, and recognized by the Bishop of the diocese as a regular auxiliary of the Church.[15]

St. Mary's Academy became the second school in the Green Bay diocese. The Sisters taught classes in both French and English, and Adele was responsible for the religious formation of the students. Quite often, the students were orphans and other children who were sent there to have a better life. The very foundation of the school rested on faith in Divine Providence, and with more than a hundred children, the tuition was only one dollar a week. Adele's goal was to make the education affordable, and so she never turned anyone away for lack of money. The single dollar did not cover all the expenses, so the sisters continued their begging tours for money, food, and other necessities.

An Impressive Visit

In 1871, the school was visited by a county school superintendent from Kewaunee, who formulated a favorable opinion from his visit:

> The main building adjacent to the chapel, is two stories high, about twenty-five by seventy feet on the ground, and is divided in the center by a hall and a stairway. Upon entering the hall, Sister Adele led the way through the right-hand doorway into the school room. The school was in charge of Sister Mary (formerly Miss Mary Gagnon of Two Rivers), a young woman of education and intelligence, who seemed well-fitted for her duties and some sixty pupils were present.
>
> Instructions were given in both French and English. … The children are generally bright looking and many of them were tolerably well advanced in their studies. … Over forty of the students are from distant localities and are boarded and cared for by the institution. Twenty-five come from Oconto alone. Only one dollar a week is charged for board and tuition. Of course, the sums received from this source are insufficient to maintain the institution and no inconsiderable part of its revenue is made up of voluntary contributions from the public.
>
> Leaving the school room, we were shown across the hall into the dining room and kitchen, and thence upstairs into the sleeping rooms which took up the entire story and corresponds in size with the two rooms below.

One is occupied by the boys and the other by the girls. In each there are some thirty low wooden cots about five feet long and two and a half feet wide; the bedding on each was neatly made up and at the foot of each was the trunk or valise of its occupant. Neither room contained any other furniture. The children are required to keep their own beds, clothing, and persons, cleanly and in order. The girls out of school are taught needlework and other useful and ornamental arts.

We left the Convent well pleased with the kind reception extended to us, and with the frankness and courtesy with which our inquiries had been answered. And, however divided the public may be in its opinion of sectarian schools, of whatever faith, or of the tenets which seem to be peculiar to this institution, we think it must be conceded the Sisters of Good Health are striving earnestly and unselfishly, for the good of their fellows as they view it, and that the children under their charge, if in afterlife they shall live in accordance with the precepts now being instilled in their minds, will be better men and women for doing so.[16]

The witness of the county superintendent paints a picture of the work and progress Adele and her companions had accomplished in such a short time. Interestingly, the Sisters in the report were referred to as "Sisters of Good Health." Whether it was with their consent to be called such or a name conferred on them by the locals is uncertain. As the Kewaunee newspaper reporter had recorded, the "physical afflictions of such as have faith are cured by the power of the Blessed Virgin, and to this circumstance is due the name of 'Good Health.'"[17] Regardless, Adele consistently referred to the chapel as Our Lady of Good Help and to herself and her companions as the Sisters of St. Francis of Assisi.[18] Records show that in 1869 the school was known as "St. Mary's Boarding Academy," and the facilities were described as under the direction of the Sisters of Good Help, a group of Franciscan Tertiaries.[19] Both the school and convent were built by the Diocese of Green Bay, yet were funded and run by Sister Adele and her companions. An article in the *Green Bay Advocate* in 1871 noted that St. Mary's Academy had already attained a "high character for usefulness and thoroughness in education and we commend it to a general patronage."[20]

Fond Memories of Former Students

An unnamed attendee of the academy's July 4, 1871 closing of the school year wrote:

> As there was to be no celebration July 4, in the city (Green Bay), we decided to go to Robinsonville, where we learned of the fourth annual exhibition at St. Mary's Academy was to take place, and the public was invited. The exercise began with a High Mass said by the Rev. Wubbels, and the Rev. P. Crud from Green Bay addressed the children. … The dialogues, the drama both in French and in the English languages were well acted.

The next year's closing ceremonies were attended by even larger crowds, evidence of the school's growing progress and achievements.[21]

First Communions were also major events at St. Mary's Academy. A former student of Sister Adele, Mrs. Theresa Gaspard, remembers the events well:

> First Communion Day was such a beautiful day. Mass at 8 o'clock. The chapel was practically filled with the Communicants. All the girls wore simple white dress-

Adele Brise in full uniform of the Sisters of St. Francis of Assisi, the community of Franciscan Tertiaries she founded. Date unknown.

1885 school and 1880 chapel. In 1869, the school would officially become St. Mary's Academy. Photo courtesy of the National Shrine of Our Lady of Good Help.

Alternate view of the 1880 Our Lady of Good help Chapel with the 1885 schoolhouse beside it. Photo courtesy of the National Shrine of Our Lady of Good Help.

Altar stone of the 1880 Our Lady of Good Help Chapel. An altar stone is a natural stone consecrated by a bishop and inserted into the surface of the altar. Typically, altar stones contain a relic of a saint. Photo courtesy of the National Shrine of Our Lady of Good Help.

Interior of the 1880 Our Lady of Good Help Chapel. Photo courtesy of the National Shrine of Our Lady of Good Help.

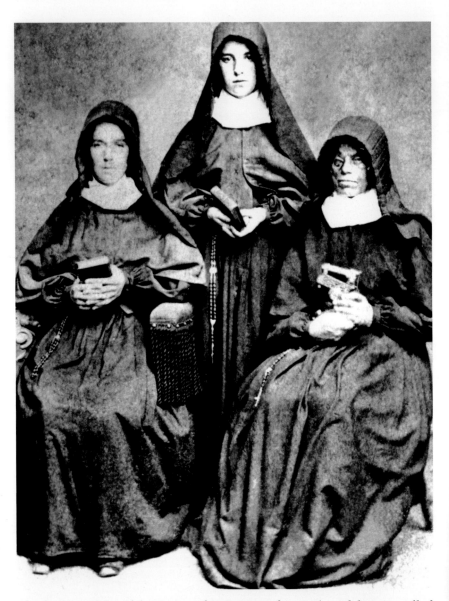

The first members of the Sisters of St. Francis of Assisi (as Adele Brise called them). The community would later become known as the Sisters of Good Health and eventually commonly known as the Sisters of Good Help. From left to right: Sister Mary Gagnon, Sister Marguerite Allard (Sister Maggie), and Sister Adele Brise. Date unknown. Photo courtesy of the National Shrine of Our Lady of Good Help.

Sister Madeleine, one of the original members of the Sisters of St. Francis of Assisi founded by Adele Brise. Date unknown. The community later was called the Sisters of Good Health or Sisters of Good Help by the locals. Photo courtesy of the National Shrine of Our Lady of Good Help.

Sister Marguerite (Maggie) Allard, one of the five original members of the Sisters of Good Help. Date unknown. Photo courtesy of the National Shrine of Our Lady of Good Help.

Sister Mary Gagnon, one of the five original members of the Sisters of Good Help. Date unknown.

Adele Brise and companions pose with the schoolchildren sometime after 1890. Adele is in the center of the photo, seated. Photo courtesy of the National Shrine of Our Lady of Good Help.

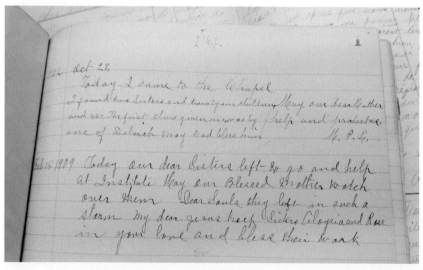

Sister Adele kept meticulous records of everything that transpired at the Chapel and school. This photo shows a 1909 ledger entry in Adele's handwriting noting the departure of two members of the community and praying for their safety.

Schoolchildren pose with three of the Sisters of Our Lady of Good Help (known by Adele Brise as Sisters of St. Francis of Assisi) in front of the 1885 school house. Date unknown. Photo courtesy of the National Shrine of Our Lady of Good Help.

Girls of Robinsonville, dressed in Sunday raiment, carry a statue of the Blessed Virgin at the head of the procession each year. It is at Robinsonville that the Catholic church maintains a school for crippled children, where special in-struction is given to the physically handicapped from adjacent territory. The procession, in which the is carried about the grounds, is participated

Schoolgirls carry the statue of Our Lady in procession on August 15, 1940. Notice the crowd in the background lining up behind them. The procession would make its way around the perimeter of the property in celebration of the Feast of the Assumption of the Blessed Virgin Mary.

Thousands Attend Field Mass at Robinsonville

ROBINSONVILLE, Wis.—Part of the thousands who attended the observance of the feast of the Assumption of the Blessed Virgin Mary here Thursday are pictured at the out-door solemn high mass celebrated by the Very Rev. Denis M.

Burke, prior of St. Norbert abbey. Four low masses were said earlier. A procession around the grounds followed. Mary visited the crippled children's home and school, conducted by the Franciscan sisters of Bay Settlement.

Newspaper clipping depicting the celebration of the Feast of the Assumption of the Blessed Virgin Mary at the Shrine of Our Lady of Good Help on August 15, 1940. Notice the headline stating that thousands of people attended. *Green Bay Press Gazette* archives, photo courtesy of the National Shrine of Our Lady of Good Help.

Pictured here in his official robes is Bishop Paul P. Rhode, of the Green Bay diocese, invoking the bless at the cornerstone laying of the new $45,000 Chapel of Our Lady of Good Help at the Crippled Children's home in R ville Tuesday afternoon. The Rev. Delbert W. Busche, diocesan chancellor, le ft, is assisting in the ceremony.

Newspaper clipping depicting the blessing of the cornerstone of the 1941 Our Lady of Good Help Chapel by Bishop Paul P. Rhode. *Green Bay Press Gazette* archives, photo courtesy of the National Shrine of Our Lady of Good Help.

Dedication of the 1941 Our Lady of Good Help Chapel. This brick chapel is the one currently at the shrine. *Green Bay Press Gazette* archives, photo courtesy of the National Shrine of Our Lady of Good Help.

The beginning of the Feast of the Assumption procession on August 15, 1943. The holy Eucharist, encased in the monstrance, is carried by the priest under the processional canopy and surrounded by altar boys carrying candles. A contingent of clergy leads the way. Photo courtesy of the National Shrine of Our Lady of Good Help.

Hundreds of people gathered at the Shrine of Our Lady of Good Help annually on August 15 to celebrate the Feast of the Assumption of the Blessed Virgin Mary. The event included holy Mass and a procession in which the statue of the Virgin Mary was carried around the perimeter of the property as the Rosary was recited. This photo from 1954 shows the length of the procession. Photo courtesy of the National Shrine of Our Lady of Good Help.

Apparition Oratory reliquary located adjacent to the Oratory statue. Left to right: Pieces of the maple and hemlock trees between which Mary stood during the apparitions, 1880 chapel altar stone, 1941 chapel altar stone. Photo by Marge Steinhage Fenelon.

Apparition Oratory Chapel built on the approximate spot of the apparitions. The statue of the Virgin Mary stands approximately where Mary stood when she appeared to Adele Brise in 1859. Directly above the statue is the altar of the 1941 chapel. Photo by Marge Steinhage Fenelon.

Reliquary containing pieces of the maple and hemlock trees between which Mary stood when she appeared to Adele Brise in 1859. Photo by Marge Steinhage Fenelon.

Closeup of the Apparition Oratory statue of the Blessed Virgin Mary. Photo by Marge Steinhage Fenelon.

Adoration in the 1941 chapel, the fourth chapel built on the apparition site.
Photo courtesy of the National Shrine of Our Lady of Good Help

Statue of Our Lady of Good Help that currently stands in Mother of Mercy Hall. Photo courtesy of the National Shrine of Our Lady of Good Help.

es. While the girls received Holy Communion the boys sang hymns. While the boys received Holy Communion the girls sang hymns. After Mass each child received a little glass of wine before their big dinner. Communion celebration lasted all day. In the afternoon they would renew their baptismal vows. Each child would have to climb onto a platform and in the presence of the whole crowd beg their parents' pardon for all their faults, or any injuries against them.[22]

Mrs. Gaspard also credits her ability to fluently speak and write both French and English to the education she received from Sister Adele. As one of the older girls, she frequently accompanied Sister Adele to the store, and each time they began praying the Rosary when they left the chapel and continued until they reached the store. If they met anyone along the way, they congenially nodded and proceeded with their prayers. There was no end of intentions for which to pray, as large numbers of people came to the chapel to ask for the prayers of Sister Adele. In response, Sister Adele would begin a procession with all the children, praying for these special intentions. It began around the tree where the Queen of Heaven appeared and around which lovely flowers had been planted.[23]

Grateful Orphans

Another testimony was given by Odile Allard, niece of Sr. Maggie Allard — one of Sister Adele's original companions. In a letter dated September 20, 1952, she wrote of her time living at St. Mary's Academy. Her mother had died when she was six years old, and consequently she and her two-and-a-half-year-old sister were placed at the school after her father realized he could not adequately care for the two little girls without their mother:

I can truly say my days with Sister Adele and her companions were happy, happy days. I've only sweet memories of those nine or ten years I spent with them. I remember well when I was about eight years old, we would pray and sing hymns around the trees where the Blessed Virgin had appeared to Sister Adele. ... I often accompanied Sister Adele on her begging tours after I was twelve and until I left. I always signed her name for her, and the names of those who would give her something; this is what makes me say she could not write. She could read a little because sometimes she would have her prayerbook at Mass, but most of the time she would have her beads. When going out begging with her, she would say the beads part of the way. I also often went with her to à la Riviere Rouge, going from house to house, asking the people to haul bricks from the river to build the new convent; very, very few would refuse.[24]

According to Allard's testimony, Sister Adele's natural sister, Isabelle, lived for a time at the school although she did not become a Franciscan tertiary. Sadly, Sister Adele found her dead in her bed one tragic morning. She also remembers an accident during which Sister Adele was thrown from the wagon after the horses had become frightened on the way to Mass at St. Joseph's Catholic Church in Bay Settlement. This incident left her with lasting injuries and physical limitations. Yet even this did not deter Sister Adele from carrying out her duties. She had her hands full teaching the more than one hundred children who boarded year-round at the school and wasted no time, even for her own recovery.

Sister Maggie was her assistant and the music teacher, dressmaker, and secretary for the school. After Sister Adele's accident, she took on many of the duties in Sister Adele's role as superior of the community, yet she did nothing without Sister Adele's permission. Sister Annie managed the kitchen, laundry, and mending the children's clothes. Allard described her as "Irish and very nice and well liked by everyone." Sister Louise was the baker, and the children loved to help her make the delicious bread and buns for which she became renowned:

> Sister Louise would bake every day, she used to bake the bread in a brick oven behind the laundry, as we called it at that time. I imagine it is all different now, but you can imagine it took some bread for so many people. We would go and help to carry the warm bread from the oven to the convent. … What sweet memories.[25]

The high point of Allard's letter was her gratitude for the gifts she had been given through her experiences at St. Mary's Academy:

> It was a real privilege from God, that I was brought up by Sister Adele; she taught us to pray, to be good, polite and obedient, she learned us to be charitable and she certainly gave us good example; it was only after I had a family of my own that I realized the good she had done me.[26] I thought then that religious life was best. I did all I could to bring up my family as she had brought me, and if I am here in this blessed home today it is to her I can look back to. There is a beginning to everything and I can say Sister Adele left her mark in my life. I often wonder how a poor girl without instruction could go to such doings without a powerful hand to guide her. She has done so much good, she was so humble, so charitable for everyone, especially for the children. The sufferings she went through in every way and manner, inclined to think and seemed to be a proof that the Blessed

Virgin has really done something, for do we not read in the lives of the saints they all went through great trials and sufferings![27]

Special Night Prayers

In an undated account, a Mrs. Herrick spoke of her time at St. Mary's Academy and in particular, the piety of Sister Adele. She explained that at night, Sister Adele would go from bed to bed on her knees praying beside the children. Sometimes, she said, the building became so cold in the winter months that some of the children slept together in twin beds to keep warm. These were hard times, yet Sister Adele never lost confidence in the Mother of God and never let the children become concerned for their own welfare.

Somehow things always worked out. For example, in the fall the farmers from the neighboring towns of Lincoln and Rosiere would collect flour, potatoes, and other vegetables in addition to pieces of calico and sheep wool for making quilts. Herrick described Sister Adele as at times seeming absent-minded or as though she had something on her mind. To her, it seemed as though Sister Adele was in constant dialogue with Our Lady. Although it is not part of the Church's apparition approval, some who frequented the chapel and school suspected that she continued to receive messages from the Queen of Heaven in the stillness of her heart.[28] Whether or not Adele Brise received any kind of locutions after the 1859 apparitions is of far less importance than the fact that she remained keen to Our Lady's wishes and relied faithfully on her intercession throughout her lifetime.

Respected by Local Clergy

And what became of the wise priest who encouraged Sister Adele in her ministry and helped to found St. Mary's Academy? Father Crud had served as the pastor of Bay Settlement for several years before he was transferred in 1871 to become pastor of St. John Catholic Church in Green Bay. Yet, no matter where his ministry took him, he never lost interest in St. Mary's Academy — the school he had helped to establish and that remained in his esteem. He frequently returned to Robinsonville, visiting the chapel and school, and he never missed a closing ceremony at the end of each school term. The reputation of the Sisters of Good Help and their work won the favor and respect not only of Father Crud, but of many of the surrounding clergy, as well as the love and admiration of the pioneers of Bay Settlement, the Door Peninsula, and beyond. No manner of difficulty or type of obstacle could keep Adele Brise from fulfilling the desires of the Queen of Heaven and honoring the will of God. This was the driving force behind everything she said or did throughout the entirety of her life, and it became the bedrock of the ministry that continues at the Shrine of Our Lady of Good Help to this day.

Chapter Nine
THE GREAT FIRE AND THE GREAT MIRACLE

Although Bay Settlement had grown in population by 1871, much of northeastern Wisconsin was still covered by dense forest, hundreds of years old. Pines grew 120 feet tall and three feet across, and the lumber from just three trees was enough to build a good-sized house. With plenty of trees, most buildings were made of wood from top to bottom, including the roof. Crude walkways and bridges were constructed of planks or split logs, and piles of logs were stacked against the houses for winter heat. The Town of Peshtigo (just across the bay) is estimated to have had about two thousand permanent residents and perhaps as many more temporary residents who came to work in the railroad, railroad-related industries, and manufacturing. It was a major center for the woodworking industry, with woodenware factories churning out wooden tubs, broom handles, clothes-pins, barrels, pails, and utensils.

Sawdust from the manufacture of these products was used to stuff mattresses and covered the streets to reduce dust and mud. Excess sawdust was piled next to the sawmills. Logs that could not be floated downriver to the mills were piled along the riverbanks. When lumberjacks cleared an area, they set fire to branches and debris and moved on to another site, while farmers burned tree stumps left after they cleared their own fields or on land they obtained from loggers when they had finished their work. Hunters made fires for warmth and cooking. In addition to these practices, railroad construction crews set fire to clear debris, and steam engines sometimes spread sparks from their smokestacks. Some of the fires were extinguished, but others were left to die out on their own. These fires continued to burn underground, destroying roots, peat, and humus, and they frequently went unnoticed to passersby. Consequently, trees toppled over from weakened roots and periodically burst into flames.[1]

These factors always posed dangers to the settlers; they were an even greater threat, however, during droughts. Such was the case through the winter, spring, and summer of 1870. The forests became severely dry, and even the most vigorous streams and rivers dried up. Forest fires cropped up and continued endlessly for weeks and months, setting the stage for the deadliest natural catastrophe in the history of America.[2]

Underground Fires

Fr. Peter Pernin, a parish priest for Peshtigo and nearby Marinette, described his experience of the dangerous underground fires while returning from a trip to visit one of his congregations. He decided to pause his journey and hunt pheasant with a local twelve-year-old boy as his guide. Although the boy claimed knowledge of the woods, the two became lost and were unable

to find their way back to the farmhouse where the priest was
lodging:

> Night was setting in, and nature was silently preparing
> for the season of rest. The only sounds audible were
> the crackling of a tiny tongue of fire that ran along the
> ground, in and out, among the trunks of the trees, leav-
> ing them unscathed but devouring the dry leaves that
> came in its way, and the swaying of the upper branches
> of the trees announcing that the wind was rising. We
> shouted loudly, but without evoking any reply. I then
> fired off my gun several times as tokens of distress. Fi-
> nally, a distant halloo reached our ears, then another,
> then several coming from different directions. Rendered
> anxious by our prolonged absence, the parents of my
> companion and the farm servants had finally suspected
> the truth and set out to seek us. Directed to our quar-
> ter by our shouts and the firing, they were soon on the
> right road when a new obstacle presented itself. Fanned
> by the wind, the tiny flames previously mentioned had
> united and spread over a considerable surface. We thus
> found ourselves in the center of the circle of fire extend-
> ing or narrowing, more or less, around us. We could
> not reach the men who had come to our assistance, nor
> could we go to them without incurring the risk of seri-
> ously scorching our feet or of being suffocated by the
> smoke. They were obliged to fray a passage for us by
> beating the fire with branches of trees at one particular
> point, thus momentarily staying its progress whilst we
> rapidly made our escape.[3]

Dangerous Storm Brewing

By September 24, fire was raging in the woods all around. Although the settlers kept watch and extinguished what fires they could, it was not enough to stop the fires that began burning at the tops of the trees and traveled above their heads. The wind was stirring and even the green leaves from the ground became swept up by the flames, forming a dense black cloud of smoke. The air carried with it a sense of impending doom.[4]

According to Father Pernin:

> Thousands of birds, driven from their roosts, flew about as if uncertain which way to go, and made the night still more hideous by their startled cries. Frequently they would fly hither and thither, calling loudly for their mates, then, hovering for a moment in the air, suddenly dart downward and disappear in the fiery furnace beneath.

By the next morning, the fires had calmed down somewhat, but toward midday the winds rose again, carrying with them flames that caught in the sawdust and timber of the town's buildings. The wind increased into a gale, scattering burning coals and cinders and setting new areas aflame. Each time, the settlers fought back with pails of water fetched from the waterways. The winds continued to increase, and fires rapidly approached the town from the west, creating blinding smoke that made it difficult to see or breathe. The people began to pack their things and move away from the areas of greatest danger. They felled trees and poured water over them, covered buildings with wet blankets to preserve them, and put out the scattered fires as they crept up. By September 27, it appeared as though things were under control and tension began to ease. Still, the people took precautions. They buried precious possessions to keep them from the flames, removed combustible materials from populated areas, and set up water hogsheads as sentinels surrounding the town to douse approaching flames. Each day, the pioneers prayed for rain, but none came.

Increasing Uneasiness

As the weekend of October 7–8 approached, the people of northeastern Wisconsin became uneasy, despite the fact that the threat of fire seemed to have abated. Father Pernin explained it this way:

> There seemed to be a vague fear of some impending though unknown evil haunting the minds of many, nor was I myself entirely free from this unusual feeling. It was rather an impression than a conviction, for, on reflecting, I saw that things looked much as usual, and arrived at the conclusion that our fears were groundless, without, however, feeling much reassured thereby.[5]

This same dread was felt among the people, not just in Peshtigo, but throughout the entire area, including Bay Settlement. Father Pernin described it as a powerlessness that no amount of reason could dissipate, plunging his faculties into listlessness.

As the afternoon of October 7 wore on, a mysterious silence overcame the land, accompanied by a dark, thickening smoke that caused an atmosphere of heavy, suffocating air. Every so often, strong gusts of wind would arise, swirl, and subside again. He wrote:

> At one time, whilst we were still in the field, the wind rose suddenly with more strength than it had yet displayed and I perceived some old trunks of trees blaze out though without seeing about them any tokens of cinder or spark, just as if the wind had been a breath of fire, capable of kindling them into a flame by its mere contact.

At about half past eight, Father Pernin observed a dense cloud of smoke overhanging the earth with a vivid red glow. Suddenly, he heard a strangely audible roaring in the distance. The air became heavy and oppressive, sapping human strength and making breathing painful and laborious. The crimson reflection in the western sky was rapidly increasing in size, and the intensity of the roaring increased as peals of thunder disrupted the silence. Then the thunder gave way to a terrible sound, like a train approaching a railroad station. Each moment, the train came nearer and nearer. The wind began increasing in violence, and the redness of the sky deepened, accompanied by the thunderous roaring.[6]

Saving the Sacred Vessels

Father Pernin hurried to the church in hopes of saving the Blessed Sacrament, sacred vessels, and the tabernacle, when suddenly a startling phenomenon caught his eye:

> It was that of a cloud of sparks that blazed up here and there with a sharp detonating sound like that of powder exploding, and flew from room to room. I understood then that the air was saturated with some special gas, and I could not help thinking if this gas lighted up from the contact with the breath of hot wind, what would it be when fire would come in actual contact with it.[7]

The air had become unfit to breathe because it was full of sand, dust, ashes, cinders, sparks, smoke, and fire. Seeing was nearly impossible for the same reasons. The townspeople, including Father Pernin, struggled to reach the river to submerge themselves in what little water was left in it. Confusion was everywhere. Father Pernin recalled:

A thousand discordant deafening noises rose on the air together. The neighing of horses, falling of chimneys, crashing of uprooted trees, roaring and whistling of the wind, crackling of fire as it ran with lightning-like rapidity from house to house — all sounds were there save that of the human voice. People seemed stricken dumb by terror. They jostled each other without exchanging look, word, or counsel. The silence of the tomb arraigned among the living; nature alone lifted up its voice and spoke.

Father Pernin was repeatedly thrown down by the force of the wind, once over a motionless object lying on the ground; it was a woman and a little girl who were both dead. The houses along the riverfront were on fire, and the wind blew flames and cinders directly into the water. It was impossible to cross to the other side since the bridge was on fire as well, and people were chaotically trying to cross in both directions. The fire was swiftly surrounding them. Father Pernin pushed his wagon into the water with the tabernacle inside and set about trying to save his own life. The others followed the priest's example by likewise jumping into the river and wading in the water. In order to keep their heads and faces from burning, they had to wet them constantly. Clothing and quilts had been thrown into the river, and these were soaked and used as covering, but they dried quickly in the furnace-like heat and caught fire as soon as they were no longer wet. The flames crossed back and forth over the river. To keep them away, the people had to continually beat the waves. By now it was around ten o'clock.[8]

Fire Tornadoes
The weather made matters worse, as a huge low-pressure cell had formed in the west at the beginning of the month. In a low-pressure system, air rises and cools off while air around the

cell rushes in to replace it, causing a counterclockwise spinning. The largest low-pressure systems are hurricanes.[9] This treacherous low-pressure system caused the blackened sky to burst into great clouds of fire. As it gained momentum, it became a thunderous fury mingled with a tornado of fire. A survivor wrote that if one could imagine the worst snowstorm ever witnessed, with each flake of coal or spark of fire driven by a terrifying wind, he would have an idea of the atmosphere when the fire struck. These fire tornadoes raced over the land, destroying everything in their paths. Buildings and people were instantly incinerated. The deadly fire made its way onto the Door Peninsula, covering the greater part of it. It ranged from Green Bay, to Lake Michigan, to what later became "Death's Door" to the north. It continued to sweep north and east and extended into parts of Outagamie, Kewaunee, Door, and Brown Counties. The firestorm annihilated town after town, including Humboldt, Green Bay, New Franken, Casco, Brussels, Rosiere, Lincoln, Robinson, and many more. The hurricane of fire widened as it advanced, and the Chapel of Our Lady of Good Help lay right in its path.[10]

Evacuate or Stay?

With fire fast approaching, Adele and her companions were faced with the critical decision of whether to evacuate or stay. They were determined not to abandon the chapel where the Blessed Mother had appeared to Adele, and they had faith that Mary would not fail to protect them. The farmers and their families from the surrounding area drove their livestock before them and raced toward the shrine. The raging inferno had encircled them entirely, and there was no means of escape. Looking behind them they saw their buildings — homes, barns, sheds — literally devoured by the fiery monster. All around them was a vast sea of fire.

Full of fear and grief, the stricken people swarmed the chapel grounds and begged the Mother of God to spare them, crying aloud in their fright. Under Adele's direction, they gathered in the chapel, reverently raised the cherished statue of Mary, and, kneeling, bore it in procession around the sanctuary. When the wind and fire nearly suffocated them, they simply turned in another direction and continued to hope while praying the Rosary. They passed the entire night this way, praying the Rosary in procession and changing direction when the heat and flames became too much to bear. "Thus passed for them the long hours of that terrible night. I know not if, supported only by nature, they would've been able to live through that awful ordeal," wrote Father Pernin.[11]

The Heavens Open

Several horrific and suspense-filled hours passed, with the people praying fervently for help from the Queen of Heaven. Suddenly, the heavens opened and delivered a downpour of rain. The fire was extinguished, but the dawn light revealed its ravages. Everything around them had been destroyed, and there were miles and miles of desolation everywhere. Nothing was left of their towns and farms, the forest had been wiped out, rivers and marshes dried up, and the incinerated bodies of people and animals lay scattered throughout. The area burned was at least fifty miles long and an average of twenty miles wide. Yet the convent, school, chapel, and the five acres of land consecrated to the Virgin Mary shone like an emerald isle in a sea of ashes. The vicious fire had licked the outside palings and left them charred. The wall of fire that had reached the chapel fence and threatened their destruction had not entered the chapel grounds. The land belonging to the Queen of Heaven had been miraculously preserved from the deadliest fire in US history. Even though it has been eclipsed by the more famous Chicago Fire that occurred on the very same night, the Peshtigo Fire was far more destructive and deadly, wiping out more than 2,400 square miles of land and taking the lives of 1,200 to 2,500 residents.[12]

Father Pernin survived the ordeal and became known as the hero of the Peshtigo Fire. Through his bravery, many lives were saved, and the tabernacle of his church was preserved. It can be viewed today in the Peshtigo Fire Museum. He visited Adele at the chapel after the Great Fire and wrote an account of his observations:

> I have no intention either of passing judgment on the apparition of the Blessed Virgin and the pious pilgrimages which have resulted from it. Ecclesiastical authority has not yet spoken on the subject; it silently allows the good work to advance, awaiting perhaps some proof more striking and irrefutable before pronouncing its fiat. Far from me be the thought of forestalling ecclesiastical judgment.
>
> I have but another word to add. If it lay within the power of any of my readers to proceed to the spot, and visit this humble place of pilgrimage, as yet in its infancy, and the only one I believe, of its nature in the United States, I earnestly counsel them to go. There, they can see and question Adele Brise who, without having sought it, is the soul and heroine of a good work, progressing with rapid strides from day to day; and I feel assured, that like myself, all those who have gone thither with an upright intention, they will return edified and happy at heart if not convinced of the reality of our Lady's apparition.[13]

There are some researchers who believe that the Peshtigo Fire was not the origin of the fire that ravaged the Bay Settlement and surrounding areas on October 8, 1871. There is evidence, however, that one or more fire tornadoes could have left the bay and continued the path of destruction. A fire tornado is caused when hot air rises from the ground and forms vertical columns or "chimneys" that then dissipate at higher altitudes. As more hot air is pulled into the rising column, it begins to swirl in a vortex similar to that which forms when water drains from the bathtub. The vortices are fed by fluids, liquids, or gases — in this case, hot air from the fires — which continue to gain momentum. One might imagine how figure skaters spin faster when they pull their arms in. The spinning vortex picks up sand, dirt, leaves, debris, and whatever else is lying on the ground. A fire tornado picks up burning embers, ash, flaming-hot gases, and flammable debris, creating a terrifying tower of flame that can extend hundreds of feet into the air. Fire tornadoes can reach temperatures of 2,000 degrees Fahrenheit (1,093 degrees Celsius), and because they move quickly, they can cut an alley of destruction for a considerable distance in just seconds and spread fires across a wide area.[14] Whether one subscribes to one opinion or the other, the fact remains that there was a fire in Bay Settlement and the surrounding area on October 8, 1871, and that just across the bay occurred the deadliest fire in US history. Both were caused by a severe Midwest drought.[15]

Most importantly, the fact remains — substantiated by a multitude of eyewitnesses — that the Chapel of Our Lady of Good Help and its accompanying land was preserved from the devastation of the Great Peshtigo Fire.

Chapter Ten
TRIALS AND PERSECUTION

Our Lord told his disciples, "Remember the word that I said to you, 'Servants are not greater than their master.' If they persecuted me, they will persecute you; if they kept my word, they will keep yours also. But they will do all these things to you on account of my name, because they do not know him who sent me" (Jn 15:20–21, NRSV). Throughout the course of history, we have seen this prophecy fulfilled in the lives of those giving witness to their Christian Faith, especially saints, religious founders, and missionaries. It was fulfilled in the life of Adele Brise as well.

News of the apparitions of the Queen of Heaven at Champion continued to spread after the fire, and the chapel became more and more a popular place for pilgrimages and religious gatherings, with growing numbers of celebrations and visits by the faithful, the skeptical, and the curious. Everyone wanted to see for themselves the spot at which the Mother of God had touched the earth. The reputation of St. Mary's Academy grew as well. Those familiar with the school knew of the sisters' vigilant and loving care of the children, the excellence of the education there, and the charity with which the Sisters of St. Francis[1] conducted their mission.

Prey to the Unscrupulous

Sadly, there were unscrupulous people who took advantage of the sisters' kindness in ways that placed a great burden on their shoulders. It was common for one or the other parent from a broken home to simply drop off two or more of their children at the boarding school door with promises of continued financial support and an advanced payment of two months tuition. After this, however, they promptly abandoned their children and never returned. The sisters also became caregivers to a large number of motherless children whose alcoholic fathers were irresponsible and unable to care for them. Adele's reputation as an outstanding educator ended up being a double-edged sword. Problem children who got out of hand at home were shipped to the chapel with the expectation that Sister Adele would set them straight. The growing number of children meant growing amounts of food and supplies were needed to house and educate them. In addition to this, the sisters also became responsible for clothing the children adequately for every kind of weather, including the rugged Wisconsin winters. As often happens with children, doctor visits, treatments, and medication were needed from time to time, and with so many children in their care, this became an added financial burden for the struggling tertiary community.

As discussed in Chapter Four, Belgians are a sociable people with a festive spirit and eager to celebrate special occasions. For the most part, their celebrations were wholesome and harmless. But the Masses and celebrations on the chapel grounds were too tempting for the avaricious pleasure-seekers, who took advantage of these gatherings to fatten their bank accounts and gratify their taste for enjoyment. A report in a local newspaper, the *Ahnapee Record*, stated:

> Many were the amusements and attractions represented; dances, games of chance, beer peddlers, tavern-keepers, and carnival attractions — all of which if mentioned would occupy a column. There were people from this county, Door, Manitowoc, and Brown; some on business and others to celebrate.[2]

This raucous revelry became particularly pronounced and problematic on the Feast of the Assumption, when hundreds of the faithful would celebrate the feast with a High Mass and Marian procession. Much to the sisters' dismay, things often got out of hand, shedding a bad light on Catholics in general, and especially on those associated with the chapel. Additionally, it strengthened the doubts and opposition of some clergy members in the vicinity who believed that Adele's story was fabricated and not a genuine Marian apparition. Consequently, the skeptical clergy felt it was their duty to report these unfortunate social gatherings to the bishop. They gave their reports to His Excellency, Most Rev. Bishop Melcher, first bishop of Green Bay (1868–73), who had no opportunity to personally visit Adele or observe her work.

Threatened with Excommunication
Archived records indicate that Bishop Melcher placed an interdict on the chapel, withheld the sacraments from Adele, and threatened her with excommunication if she persisted in telling

her story of the apparitions. Knowing her innocence and convinced of the authenticity of what she had seen, Adele continued to attend Sunday Mass with the children at St. Joseph's Church, a mile west of the chapel. It is told that on one occasion she found the pews blocked to her entry, and so she participated in Holy Mass kneeling in the aisle the whole time. When it was time for holy Communion, she humbly but resolutely approached the Communion rail. If she were unable to receive the Eucharist — her source of strength and courage — then it would not be of her own accord. By the grace of God, the priest gave her Communion, and her soul was filled with a new courage and resolve. This was just the first in a series of occasions in which her obedience caused her much hardship and heartache.[3]

Eventually, Bishop Melcher decided to investigate matters himself and planned to visit the chapel. When news of this reached the ears of the vendors and rabble-rousers, they immediately registered strong protests and somehow convinced the bishop to change his mind. Instead, he wrote to Adele, commanding her to dismiss the children, lock the school and chapel, and bring him the keys.[4] This placed Adele in a formidable situation because it was impossible to immediately comply with Bishop Melcher's orders. She could not merely close the school and leave. At that time, there were more than sixty children in residence, and transportation was both crude and unreliable. The roadways were yet undeveloped and the only means of transport was a horse, stagecoach, or buggy. Getting the children from the chapel to Green Bay — a distance of sixteen miles — would be a major expedition. The sisters owned no horses or buggies, and so they were forced to depend upon the stagecoach, which could accommodate only a limited number of people at a time. The stagecoach ran three times a week and did not coincide with train schedules, causing interruptions in their journeys. Occasionally they could accompany a neighboring farmer on his way to the city, but this was not something they could consistently rely on. On top of this, they needed to notify the parents of these children and secure travel expenses for them ahead of time, since the sisters had no money to pay the fares themselves. Already during the preceding months, Adele had sent hundreds of letters pleading, begging, and at times even threatening to return the children to parents who were months delinquent in paying tuition. The bishop's instruction only made matters worse. Archived reports, however, show that somehow Adele managed to buy a piece of property near the chapel in order to build a home where she could continue housing and educating the children after she had given the keys to the bishop.

The moment came when Adele met with Bishop Melcher to hand the keys over to him. In the process, she reminded him that he would be responsible for the souls lost due to the lack of instruction in the Faith because of his decision. It is said that he was so impressed with Adele's zeal and sincerity that he promptly returned the keys to her and counseled her to continue her good work.[5]

Petty Quarrels and Misunderstandings

As we know, priests were scarce in the Belgian community, and as human nature would have it, not all were model pastors. Despite this drawback, several churches were built in the area. Nevertheless, petty quarrels and misunderstandings led to the laity's unwillingness to support Catholic schools. One aspect of these church battles involved changing attitudes toward the chapel. The attitude of many of the locals shifted, and they now saw it as a bewildering problem somehow competing or conflicting with the development of the individual parishes. These arguments and complaints reached the attention of the diocesan administrator, and he lost no time in dealing with the situation. The matters were reported to the new bishop, Most Rev. Francis Xavier Krautbauer, shortly after he arrived in Green Bay on July 2, 1875.

Three weeks later, Bishop Krautbauer, accompanied by his vicar general, the Very Rev. Edward Daems, went unannounced to appraise the situation at the chapel. Caught unawares and unprepared, Adele and her companions were visibly upset and highly disturbed by this. It is likely that this was reflected in the bishop's assessment. The day after the bishop's visit, Adele wrote him a letter of apology for the seeming impoliteness on the part of the sisters during his visit and included a pleading request to know why they had been excommunicated as they understood it.

The letter reads in part:

> Some people came here this morning when they heard about your visit yesterday, and there was a kind of excitement when they knew that your Lordship was accompanied by the Rev. Daems instead of the good pastors who could give better information. ... For if the last of your children, we will also be the most respectful and the most obedient of all, even in the case of condemnation by your Lordship. ... In the name of our dear Mother, let us know the crime we have committed.[6]
>
> If we are allowed to continue the hard task we undertook with the approbation of two right reverend bishops and under the direction of several good pastors. We will try to do just as well as before our sad misfortunes. We do not want to promise better. Now dear and Right Rev. Bishop, if your Lordship wants some explanation about the apparition of our dear Mother in this holy place, about the many miracles wrought in the chapel, about the immense crowd of pilgrims who came to pray with us, we are ready to give them.[7]

The Ban Is Lifted

It is not known exactly when the ban was lifted nor the misunderstandings cleared, but eventually, St. Mary's Academy was again flourishing, and pilgrimages had resumed. Sister Pauline said about this phase of Adele's mission:

> Dear Sister had a great deal to suffer from some misunderstandings, especially from some of the clergy; but all this was to make her feel that this is not our true home, and she took it in good faith. I never heard her say an unkind word against them. She was always charitable and obedient. Her work prospered as she did a great deal of good.[8]

The Catholic Church is extremely cautious concerning private revelations or reported visions from heaven, and this shows necessary prudence. The Church must always defend the truth and be ever alert against deception. Over the centuries, there have been a myriad of reports of false apparitions, and the Church must be careful to discern what is real and worthy of belief or contrived so that the faithful are not misled. For this reason, the clergy who questioned or opposed Adele Brise should not be criticized. Besides the disturbances of the disorderly and impious festivities held on the chapel grounds, other graver abuses were taking place nearby. The evil one will stop at nothing in his attempts to destroy the works of God, and by his devilish means, villains fell into spite and hatred for what Catholics hold sacred. Again, Adele was not responsible for the mockery and abuses that took place near the chapel or parish churches, but somehow it put her in a bad light and further tainted her reputation.

Rise of the Spiritualists

An even greater spiritual storm was brewing in Green Bay; however, one that would seriously erode the faith of Catholics in the area. The wife of a Belgian saloon keeper named John B. Everts became extremely ill. After several doctors failed to cure her, Everts was directed to a spiritualistic medium who claimed he had the gift of healing. Strangely, Mrs. Everts responded to the spiritualist's treatments and finally recovered her health. Upon being paid for his services, the spiritualist proclaimed that Mr. Everts, too, had the gift of healing and urged him to sell his business and become a spiritualist himself.

Impressed with this compliment, Mr. Everts sold his business and entered the dangerous world of spiritualism, holding séances in private houses that attracted many. This came to the attention of the local priest, who discredited the spiritualist, declaring that no medium could converse with the dead if he interposed. A Belgian businessman by the last name of Duchateau heard this and offered to bet the priest one thousand dollars that he could not make good on his claim. The priest accepted the challenge, and a contest was set for June 22, 1885. Practically the entire town gathered at the appointed time to witness the duel of supernatural powers. However, the priest did not show up at the appointed time, and a messenger was sent to his house with a horse and buggy to get him. He was home but unwilling to go and claimed that he was not yet fully prepared. In view of the circumstances, however, the priest finally consented and returned with the messenger. Those who had come to see a spectacle were disappointed, for the priest refused to have anything to do with this "infernal business" and instead berated all who were present for listening to heretics' deviltries and false prophets. This incident resulted in a great victory for the spiritualists, and about forty families left the Catholic Church and built a non-Catholic church of their own.[9]

A Heretical Sect Forms

Soon yet another gentleman presented with supernatural healing powers and the ability to communicate with spirits. A group known as the Gardner Spiritualists formed, and their notoriety spread throughout the region. With the introduction of occult practices to the area, religious confusion and unrest grew. A new spiritual leader named Joseph Rene Vilatte emerged. Formerly a French Presbyterian minister, he became aware that Belgians were generally opposed to Presbyterianism. So, he decided to become an ordained Catholic priest as part of a schismatic and heretical European sect known as Old Catholics that did not adhere to the Magisterium of the Catholic Church.

Unable to obtain ordination from any bishops in America, Vilatte went to Switzerland and was ordained there as an Old Catholic bishop. Upon returning to Wisconsin, he put himself under the authority of the Episcopalian bishop in Fond du Lac and carried on his work among the Belgians of the Bay Settlement area. Vilatte was a gifted speaker with a charismatic persona and was able to convince many Catholics that the Catholic Church was just as erroneous as the Spiritualists.[10] He traveled about the Door Peninsula spreading his heresies and gathering a significant following, especially among unsuspecting, unhappy, and under-catechized Catholics. Eventually, Vilatte managed to build four churches within a one-mile radius of the Chapel of Our Lady of Good Help. Under his guidance, the Old Catholic church became more progressively Protestant, denying compulsory confession, the Immaculate Conception, indulgences, and clerical celibacy, and introducing Mass in the vernacular, which was not yet allowed by the Magisterium.[11]

The previous troubles between clergy and laity in the Catholic community fostered the dissemination of false doctrines. The

United States indeed harbored troublesome characters and rebellious parishes, but neither dreamed of becoming "Old Catholics" because the background was lacking. It took fifteen years
for that movement to infect America, and then it was used to
deceive the unlettered and to flatter the ambitions of renegades.
The stage for this was the Belgian settlement in Wisconsin.[12]
Lukewarm Catholics were pleased with Vilatte's "revised" religion because it was so easy to live by. Thus it spread rapidly in
the peninsula and eventually obtained a foothold in Green Bay.

This strange "bishop" gravely concerned Adele. A former
student of the chapel during this time wrote, "The so-called
Bishop Vilatte came and settled not far from the chapel. I mention this because Sister Adele would take us to the chapel and
make us pray that he would not do harm; he was still there when
I left (1887)." Vilatte and his followers caused a great deal of ag-
itation against the work done at the chapel and used the earlier
accusations that had been leveled against Adele to discredit the
Catholic Church in the eyes of the public. The threat of the "Old
Catholic" heresy concerned Green Bay Bishop Sebastian Geb-
hard Messmer as well. He wrote to the Norbertine Superior of
the Abbey of Berne in Holland requesting missionary priests to
help combat the heretical sect. In November 1893, Fr. Bernard
Pennings, Fr. Lambert Broems, and Br. Servatius Heesackers arrived in the town of Delwiche, which was the heart of the troubled district. Others followed in time, and this was the humble
beginning of the Norbertine Order in America. [13]

Beseeching Mary's Protection

Soon after his arrival, Father Pennings initiated a pilgrimage
from his parish and missions on the last Monday in May. This
became a tradition among the Catholic parishes on the peninsula. The purpose of the pilgrimage was to beseech Mary's help
and protection against the evil work and influence of Vilatte. The

"bishop" found out about this, and when the pilgrimage passed his residence at the town of Duvall in their wagons, Vilatte himself stood along the road behind a table on which he had placed a statue of the Blessed Virgin Mary with candles and flowers. It is interesting to note the blatant inconsistencies of this heretic concerning the veneration of the Mother of God. Had he not instructed his congregations to cease their devotion to Mary?

Vilatte was somehow appointed as "archbishop," and in 1896 he appointed a Rev. Mr. Miller as pastor of the Old Catholic church in Green Bay. A year later, Miller was forced to resign because his congregation would not abide by the Old Catholic reforms (the introduction of public confession instead of private confession and abolishing devotion to Mary). In his own defense, Miller wrote:

> I labored for the much-needed reform, and I sought to carry out Archbishop Vilatte's commission to do the best for the local church. … Somehow the notion had gained ground that now the Church was not Old Catholic but Protestant. Then I called a meeting of the congregation to be held after Vespers for free discussions of the questions involved. … It was now found that the congregation would not get along without the altar of the Virgin Mary. In view of this and certain other facts I resigned.[14]

The Norbertines continued their valiant efforts to strengthen the faith of those who had not been led astray and to win back those who had fallen into the grasp of the heretical Vilatte. The unrelenting labors of Father Pennings and his companions over five long years bore so much fruit that the *Catholic Citizen* reported on February 19, 1898, that "Vilatte, Primate of the Old Catholic Church in America, has been left flockless, churchless and landless. The mighty shepherd has been deprived of his sheep hold (*sic*) and his little flock have sought more congenial pastures."[15]

Never once throughout all the trials and persecutions did Adele's trust in the Queen of Heaven waver. Never once did she forget the message she received on October 8, 1859, nor deviate from the mission given her that day. She was and always remained impeccable in her obedience to God's will and the authority of the Church, heroically bearing painful crosses for herx sake. Perhaps in the darkest moments of tribulation, she recalled Our Lord's words to his disciples, "If they persecuted me, they will persecute you."

Adele could see the beautiful lady, clothed in dazzling white with a yellow sash around her waist. Her dress fell to her feet in graceful folds, and she had a crown of twelve stars around her head. Her long, golden, wavy hair fell loosely over her shoulders, and such a heavenly light shone around her that Adele could hardly look at her sweet face. Overcome, Adele fell to her knees.

She dared to speak to the lady. "In God's name, who are you and what do you want of me?" she asked. The beautiful lady replied, "I am the Queen of Heaven who prays for the conversion of sinners, and I wish you to do the same. You received Holy Communion this morning and that is well. But you must do more. Make a general confession and offer Communion for the conversion of sinners. If they do not convert and do penance, my Son will be obliged to punish them."

The Lady continued, "What are you doing here in idleness while your companions are working in the vineyard of my Son?"

"What more can I do, dear Lady?" Adele asked, weeping.

"Gather the children in this wild country and teach them what they should know for salvation," the Queen of Heaven instructed.

Chapter Eleven
FULFILLING ADELE'S MISSION

A dele and her companions gave the best years of their lives in service to the Queen of Heaven at the Chapel of Our Lady of Good Help in Champion (Robinsonville). The first group included Sr. Mary Gagnon, the school's first teacher. Records do not indicate how long she was at the Chapel; however, they do show that she was there with the opening of the first school in 1867 and was one of the signers of the letter written to Bishop Krautbauer in July 1875. In 1870, Sr. Marguerite Allard (affectionately called Sister Maggie) joined the community and was Sister Adele's capable assistant and loyal coworker for twenty years. About the same time, Sister Maggie's natural sister, Addie, joined the community and became a teacher as well. Together the biological sisters played a key role in the growth and development of the shrine and school. As previously mentioned, Sister Annie saw to all the kitchen, laundry, and mending duties for the community and the children, and Sister Louise was the proficient baker who warmed the hearts and stomachs of the children with her delectable baked goods. These five holy and courageous women bore the responsibilities, hardships, and exhausting labors required for laying the foundation of a mighty work of God.

Franciscan Tertiaries

The Catholic Almanac refers to these women under various titles: Quasi Sisters of the Third Order of St. Francis, Community of Young Ladies, "Beguines," and Secular Franciscan Sisters. These names demonstrate uncertainty about their ecclesiastical classification. The last designation, however, seems most fitting, since they called each other "Sister," which is common among Tertiary Seculars. The term *Beguine* was applied to pious gatherings or associations of unvowed women who came together for the purpose of prayer and good works. These groups were commonly found in Germany, Belgium, and Holland, as well as northeastern France, especially in the Middle Ages. In the fifteenth century, there was an attempt to include them in the newly sanctioned Mendicant Orders,[1] because Beguine communities often held heretical ideas that were generated among them. Recall, though, that Sister Adele and her companions did not belong to any religious order or congregation, took no vows, retained their property and independence, and were free to leave whenever they wished. They dressed as the Franciscans did and lived in community but did not undergo a novitiate before joining. This, of course, left the door open to the possibility that members could suddenly depart, leaving the other sisters shorthanded.

At the time Sister Adele formed the Sisters of St. Francis, there seems to have been a springtime of such tertiary communities in central and northeastern Wisconsin. Records were not kept of Tertiary Seculars prior to 1920, and so it is not documented who received the young Belgian women into the Church as tertiaries. However, there is record of a letter written in 1889 by Sr. Marie Madeleine, in which she said, "I, Marie, was received last year with several other girls in the Order of St. Francis of Assisi."[2] Given that these women were bound together only by their love of the Blessed Mother and fervency for the mission she gave to Adele, the immense contribution they made to education and the Faith is remarkable.

Building of the Third Chapel

Bishop Krautbauer never officially recognized Adele's story or alleged apparitions, but he did give pastoral sanction to erect a larger Chapel, school, and convent to meet new demands. New buildings were desperately needed, but the people in the area Adele served were very poor. After prayerful reflection, Adele, confident in the help of the Queen of Heaven, resolved to again beg for funds. Twenty-two priests led by Bishop Krautbauer, including such names as Father J. Fox, a future Bishop of Green Bay, as well as other prominent priests of the diocese, contributed toward the building fund. This secured the building of the third Chapel, which this time would be made of brick:

> The great work she hoped to accomplish, for the undertaking of which she labored and was willing to suffer anything, would serve as a crown for her efforts, and in some way as the approval of the mission which she claimed was given her.
>
> Work began in 1880. The Chapel, home of Our Lady of Good Help, was to be built first. The plans for both Chapel and home were made by the Most Rt. Rev. Krautbauer, then Bishop of Green Bay.[3]

The new school, dormitory, and convent were completed in 1885. The *Green Bay Advocate* printed the following observation of the completion and dedication of the chapel. "Bishop Kraut-bauer, assisted by several priests, formally dedicated by his solemn blessing the new chapel at Robinsonville a few days since. High Mass was sung, and the Bishop made an address."[4] Even this Ccapel was eventually outgrown for the hordes of visitors each year, and so it was razed in 1941 to make way for the construction of the present one.

During the razing and construction of the new chapel, the two stumps of the trees at which the apparitions took place were found beneath the floor of the sanctuary. The altar in the current chapel is believed to have been built above the spot where the stumps were discovered.[5] A statue of Mary holding the Child Jesus was donated in 1942 by Fr. Rudolph Hodik, pastor of Holy Trinity Parish in Casco, and placed above the altar.[6] Beneath the chapel, a crypt was dug and made into an underground grotto in the place where the trees' roots would have grown. In the crypt, a statue depicting Mary as Our Lady of Grace stands directly below the statue of Mary in the Chapel and above the reported site where the Queen of Heaven appeared to Adele. The statue was brought from France in 1907 by Fr. Philip Crud and donated for the crypt.[7] The crypt, now known as the Apparition Oratory, is a quiet place of prayer where the presence of Mary can be experienced by visitors. Cases in the oratory contain artifacts of the Chapel's history, including small pieces of wood said to have been preserved from the maple and hemlock trees where Mary appeared to Adele. In 2013, Green Bay Bishop David Ricken commissioned a local artisan to create a statue of the Queen of Heaven as Adele had described her. The commissioned statue of Mary as she appeared to Adele has been moved to the back of the Mother of Mercy Hall.[8]

Annual Pilgrimages Begin

Pilgrimages to the Chapel have been conducted continuously since 1861. When one considers the obstacles to travel and dissemination of news in those early days, most likely the pilgrims came mainly from the Door Peninsula and the area around Green Bay. After the school was established, the news of the apparitions spread more broadly, and pilgrims came from a much wider region. While there had already been a steady increase in the number of pilgrims, the number increased exponentially after the miraculous preservation of the land during the Great Fire of 1871.

The February 22, 1878, issue of the *Kewaunee Enterprise* contained an article about the pilgrimages, stating:

> Annually on August 15, the festival of the Assumption of the Blessed Virgin Mary is celebrated here with imposing ceremonies, and the image of the Virgin is taken from the Chapel and carried in procession which usually numbers thousands — the people gathering on this occasion from Door, Kewaunee, Brown, Oconto, and adjoining counties.

The hand-carved statue of the Blessed Mother originally carried in the processions was imported from Belgium. It arrived in Dykesville, not far from Robinsonville, on the Denessen steamer.[9] It was then carried in a grand procession to the chapel with hymns and prayers sung along the way. The procession concluded by encircling the chapel grounds, and the statue was placed on the chapel altar. Histories show that this was the first of innumerable such processions that continue to our present day.

Fire Strikes Again

An unfortunate accident occurred during one of the early processions when a gust of wind caused the lighted candles to ignite the decorations surrounding the statue, marring it beyond repair.[10] It was replaced with a statue that had been brought from Belgium by Fr. Edward Daems in 1853 and placed in Holy Cross Catholic Church at Bay Settlement, where Adele attended Mass before the founding of St. Joseph's Catholic Church in Robinsonville (Champion). It was before this same statue that she knelt and prayed with the very first groups of children she had catechized and prepared for the sacraments. Sometime between 1864 and 1870, Father Daems gave the statue as a gift to Fr. Philip Crud, pastor of the new St. Joseph's Catholic Church from 1867–1870. It remained there until 1908 when Norbertine Fr. Milo Smits became the new pastor and donated the statue to the chapel. In 1953, the statue was given a wig of human hair. The hair came from Sr. Regina LaMere, a member of the Sisters of St. Francis of the Holy Cross. Because she was so positively influenced by Sr. Alphonsus Jabobe, her teacher in fourth through sixth grades, she entered the community at age fifteen. Sister Alphonsus had asked her to grow her hair until she entered the postulancy, and so on August 12, 1943, Sister Regina's hair was cut and put aside for the statue.[11] The new statue was smaller and lighter in weight than the original one, making it easier to carry in processions.[12]

Another account given in the *Kewanee Enterprise* on August 25, 1878, described the immensity of the annual celebrations at the chapel on the Solemnity of the Assumption of the Blessed Virgin Mary:

> The preceding day hundreds of pilgrims were on the spot, camping in the open air around the venerated sanctuary. … Four grand processions had come under the leadership of their respective pastors. One from the Holland Church in Green Bay; another from Luxembourg and other nearby places; and the third from Dykesville and Grandlez. The three processions went to meet that

of Robinsonville. After that, High Mass commenced followed by sermons given in French, Holland, and English. Horsemen wearing sashes around their shoulders opened the procession; then chants and prayers in different languages, the floating banners, young girls clad in white carrying the statue of the Virgin; five priests in sacerdotal ropes followed, and the discharge of cannon at intervals was an unforgettable sight.[13]

In 1879 it was estimated that there were thousands of groups on the grounds for the celebration of the Assumption. Three Masses were said, and homilies preached in five different languages: French, German, English, Dutch, and Bohemian. In addition to those who came by horse and buggy, throngs more came on foot or by water. Of these celebrations, Sister Madeleine wrote in a letter to her aunt:

> The day of the Assumption of the Blessed Virgin Mary, August 15, is a great feast here in our Chapel at our Convent. Thousands of pilgrims from all over assisted at these beautiful ceremonies. Mass was sung at 10:00 AM after which a sermon was delivered by Rev. Father Lebras, and the procession was held accompanied by priests, Sisters and thousands of people.[14]

The celebrations on the Solemnity of the Assumption of the Blessed Virgin Mary continue to occur at the shrine.

Bishop Blocks Celebrations

In 1926, greed once again reared its ugly head among those who saw an opportunity to make money on the Assumption celebrations, and commercialization of the events caused a serious problem. That year, Green Bay Bishop Paul Peter Rhode ordered the celebrations to be discontinued. An August 1926 article in the *Green Bay Advocate* recounted: "The reasons stated in general as given by the prelate, were to the effect that unworthy persons had made the occasion one for the sale of liquor, contrary to the laws of the United States (Prohibition) and that it was bringing disgrace upon the Blessed Mother and the Church."[15] Patricia Boerschinger, whose family lived near the Chapel and visited it often, remembers the closing without hard feelings against Bishop Rhode. "It was too much of a circus atmosphere," she said. "It (Solemnity of the Assumption) was meant to be a holy thing, but these people took away from that. I can understand why the bishop closed it even though it made us sad."[16]

Despite the bishop's orders, people continued to make private pilgrimages to the Chapel while, thankfully, the objectionable behavior ceased. Two years later, the religious celebrations resumed when Father Smits, the Chapel's appointed chaplain, was able to purchase the surrounding land that had been rented by the scoundrels for commercial purposes. It cost him upwards of one thousand dollars an acre — an exorbitant price in those days — but worth it to assure the sacredness of the Chapel grounds and the continuation of the feast day celebrations.

The Gate Reopens

With the gate now opened, the Assumption celebrations increased in size and holy festivities, and by the summer of 1954, at least 15,000 pilgrims came for the great feast on August 15. Green Bay had a new bishop by this time, the Most Rev. Bishop Stanislaus Vincent Bona, who took great interest in the Chapel, and under his inspiring leadership, large parish groups from throughout the state came with their pastors to honor the Queen of Heaven. Additionally, large groups from schools, clubs, academies, churches, and various societies heeded the pleas of Pope Pius XII. Daily, people were seen devotedly kneeling around the throne of Our Lady of Good Help and circling the altar on their knees while praying the Rosary. Especially on August 15, this holy traffic went on continuously from 4:30 AM until 9:30 PM. To accommodate the large crowds, Mass was held outdoors, and the bishop was asked to officiate. Thousands of pilgrims stood in the fields, along the fences, and against the buildings even in the humid heat of the Wisconsin summer. Vehicles of all kinds lined the roadsides, seemingly for miles. Even skeptics sensed the pervading religious atmosphere. At the conclusion of Mass, the procession wound its way around the Chapel grounds led by a crucifer, and the statue of the Queen of Heaven carried by four girls. The crowds of pilgrims lined up ten or more abreast, praying the Rosary accompanied by the clergy and the Blessed Sacrament.[17]

Reports of Miracles

It was not only the fine reputation of the Sisters of St. Francis that attracted the multitudes to the chapel, it was also the many reports of miracles that happened either on the pilgrimage route or at the chapel itself. Patricia Boerschinger recalled that, during her childhood, people walked to the chapel from long distances. "People walked from all over the country, and it's surprising how far they'd come from. Mary obviously was at work there," she said.[18] To be clear, all the miracles reported are anecdotal in nature, in the sense that they have not been authenticated by the Church. Miracles confirm the reality of the supernatural and reassure us of God's existence. Clearly those who seek miracles at the chapel are convinced of that reality.

The Church, however, has a strict procedure for examining each event and determining whether it was of "supernatural origin." One of the most common types of miracles is the sudden healing of someone, and this has been the case with the bulk of the miracles attributed to the chapel. As Miracle Hunter Michael O'Neill stated in an article for Aleteia:

For the cure to be considered miraculous, the disease must be serious and impossible (or at least exceedingly difficult) to cure by human means and not be in a stage at which it is liable to disappear shortly by itself. No medical treatment must have been given, or it must be certain that the treatment given has no reference to the cure. The healing must be spontaneous, complete and permanent.

In all cases, the local bishop is the first to investigate the alleged miracle, with the help of a board of medical professionals. More often than not, an alleged miracle is not verified.[19] But for those who received miracles from the Queen of Heaven and those who were confident in the Champion apparitions and Mary's continued presence there, there was no need of proof. The numbers of crutches, canes, and braces were evidence enough.[20]

An undated story is told of the five-year-old niece of Sisters Maggie and Addie, who was kicked in the face by a horse. When the mother saw the limp body of her little daughter and saw the blood draining from her little body, she spontaneously promised to make a pilgrimage on foot to the chapel, a distance of twelve miles. The bleeding stopped instantly. The little girl suffered no internal injuries nor physical defects, which was considered a miracle. Eventually, she became a religious in another community and spent her life serving God as a bride of Christ.[21]

Fr. Adalbert Cipin, a Czech pastor in the Bay Settlement area, kept a chronicle of his four parishes. In it, he describes how he would take groups of parishioners from the different churches on pilgrimage to the chapel. On one occasion, in 1887, he witnessed the inexplicable recovery of a thirty-five-year-old man deep in the throes of diphtheria.[22] His condition was severe, and he went to seek a cure from the Mother of God. He was confident that she would grant his petition. The man was so sick that he was taken directly to the convent upon his arrival, where Sister Adele tended to him while Father Cipin took care of the pilgrims. In the interim, the man's condition became desperate, and it looked as if there was no hope. As a last resort, Sister Adele and Father Cipin, with great difficulty, sought to help him by blowing sulfur powder into his throat through a paper tube forced between his teeth.[23] It did not help. As his attention was pulled in many directions that day, Father Cipin had to briefly leave the convent. Minutes later, he heard the man's wife wailing in mourning, begging the assistance of Our Lady of Good Help. It seemed the man had died in the priest's absence. When he reached the convent, Father Cipin found the man sitting at the dining room table, drinking tea, eating, and breathing easily as if he had never fallen ill. He cheerfully greeted Father Cipin and said, "For this I went on pilgrimage, that the Virgin Mother would heal me."[24]

On August 15, 1954, a gentleman wearing a hearing aid approached a woman leading the group Rosary during the procession. She indicated to him on her rosary the correct place, and he went back to his spot in the procession. About halfway around the path, the gentleman removed his hearing aid. Before he entered the chapel at the end of the procession, the woman stepped back and said, "Thank you for saying the Rosary with us." He replied, "Thank you, and thank God I can now hear."[25]

Another time, the same woman gave the report of an instant cure that she had witnessed as a girl when she had attended school at St. Mary's Academy (while Sister Adele was still alive). A blind child was brought to the chapel by his mother. It was not unusual for the petitioners to ask Sister Adele to join with them in prayer. On the occasions when she was unable to do so, she would appoint several of the schoolgirls to say the Rosary with the pilgrims, and in this case, she designated the woman (Josie) to lead it. During the recitation of the Rosary, there were shouts from the child in his mother's arms. Pointing in various directions, the child cried, "Mama look! Mama look!" He could see.[26]

More recently was the 2017 healing of a man who was incapable of walking due to a crippling condition that affected his legs. During a Healing Mass — an event celebrated on a regular basis at the Shrine — he suddenly bolted up and ran to the priest who was conducting the healing service. The priest was Fr. Ubald Rugirangoga, a priest from the Diocese of Cyangugu, Rwanda, who had been granted the gift of healing. Father Ubald, who passed away in January 2021, has won worldwide acclaim for his ministry of forgiveness in the wake of the Rwandan genocide. He was a frequent visitor to the Shrine of Our Lady of Good Help because he could feel Mary's presence there. As he so often told congregations during his homilies there, he considered it an important place of grace.[27]

The physical healings pale in comparison to the untold numbers who have experienced conversion and transformation. Hardened sinners have changed their ways, and nonbelievers have come to believe. The fallen away have returned to the Church, many after decades-long absences. Those suffering deep sorrow and distress have experienced consolation and peace. Priests hear hours of confessions after every Mass, and the number of conversions that take place during these confessions is impressive. More about this is included in the final chapter of this book, but for now suffice it to say that miracles of spiritual healing were a prominent part of the proliferation of the Chapel and Sister Adele's work there.

Deadly Croup Epidemic

Lamentably, the growth and expansion brought with it yet more sufferings for Sister Adele in the last years of her life. In 1890, an epidemic of deadly croup[28] swept through the school and convent, and on the first of January it claimed the lives of two children just a few hours apart. They were buried in the little cemetery beside the Chapel, and Sister Adele had to face the heartbreaking task of explaining this travesty to the parents. Others contracted the disease, and the doctor ordered the rest of the children home for a month's vacation. As we know from Sister Adele's experience transporting the children after the bishop's temporary closing of the institution in 1868, the task of transporting more than one hundred children was a costly and complicated one. As before, she managed to get them all home safely. By an act of Providence, the children were on their way back to the school by the middle of February.

Sister Maggie Dies

On February 15, 1890, Adele suffered a tremendous loss when Sister Maggie — her greatest help and support — became seriously ill. On February 27, she died a holy death, promising in her last moments to pray for the Sisters and their mission in heaven. Sister Adele wrote of her:

> Sister Maggie left a great vacancy in our Convent, and it is a separation extremely hard to take. She was here twenty years with us, and she has always been so faithful to me, as a good child towards her mother. But we must bow to God's Holy Will.[29]

After Sister Maggie died, the convent and school were gripped by a general decline. For some years, Sister Adele had been of poor health and was unable to carry out the responsibilities of convent superior and school administrator. Therefore, she placed the management of the home in the hands of a young sister who had attended school there and had entered their community in 1888. The older members who had served with Sister Adele since the early years became discouraged by the state of affairs and were obviously unhappy about the changes. More than half of them left

all at once, putting Sister Adele in a precarious situation. She had
not anticipated this, and it grieved her. She wept bitterly, realizing
that putting a younger sister in charge was a mistake. However,
even this did not cause her to lose faith in God or decrease her
trust that he had permitted this with good reason. Since this was
his work, it would somehow continue.

The Death of Sister Adele

Tragically, extinction of the Sisters of St. Francis seemed immi-
nent with the approach of Sister Adele's death. The community had dwindled to three, and the school greatly diminished in
the number of students enrolled. It seemed as though Our Lord
were asking Adele to endure one last round of terrible suffering.
Still, she did not lose her peace of soul, nor did she falter in her
total submission to his divine will. As Reverend R. Greven wrote
in his book, *I Am the Queen of Heaven: The Story of the Chapel
at Robinsonville, Wisconsin,*

> She lingered long, but the last week she spoke little. The
> Rev. Lambert Broens, P. Praems gave her the sacraments
> of the dying and later he was wont to tell what an edify-
> ing spectacle Sister Adele's deathbed was.
>
> In the little graveyard beside her dear Chapel, Sister
> Adele was laid to rest. A very simple tombstone bears
> the following inscription in French, which we translate
> for our readers:

Sacred Cross, under thy shadow
I rest and hope.
Sister Marie Adele Joseph Brice
Died July the 5th, 1896.
At the age of 66 years.[30]

According to an account given by Fr. Milo Smits, who became pastor of St. Joseph Catholic Church in Robinsonville in 1908, Father Broens was convinced of the authenticity of Adele's account of the apparitions of the Blessed Virgin Mary in Champion (Robinsonville), Wisconsin, on October 9, 1859. Furthermore, he was convinced that she was of sound mind and not capable of hallucinations. In his observation, she had never claimed that the apparitions were due in any way to merit on her part, nor did she seek any recognition for it. Throughout her life, she remained an unpretentious character.[31] Until her final breath, Adele was an outstanding example of obedience, piety, holiness, faith, trust in God's will, missionary zeal, and devotion to the Queen of Heaven. Her only ambition was to fulfill the mission Our Lady had given her, and for this singular goal, she spent all her strength.

Chapter Twelve
SISTERS OF ST. FRANCIS OF THE HOLY CROSS

Due to the lack of leadership and declining number of children and resources, the situation at the chapel steadily worsened. Without the leadership and assurance of Sister Adele and the able assistance of Sister Maggie, the remaining members of the community floundered. Aware of the sad circumstances, Bishop Messmer went to the chapel to appraise the status of the institution. Much to his alarm, he found woeful conditions and a general state of disarray. There were outstanding bills, dire want, and no credit. Conditions were inadequate to the point that he felt the need to act promptly. He advised the three remaining women to join the Sisters of St. Francis of Assisi of the Holy Cross at Bay Settlement if they desired to continue the lifestyle of a religious. Either that or return to secular occupations and forge a new life for themselves elsewhere. In 1902, the acting Superior, Sister Madeleine, decided to leave the community and pursue a new life in the secular world.[1]

Introduction of the Sisters

It is important to note that the Sisters of St. Francis of the Holy Cross were formed by a group of four women under the direction of Fr. Edward Daems and chronologically parallel to the Sisters of St. Francis of Assisi founded by Adele Brise. Around 1868, they began as a Third Order of St. Francis with the primary mission of teaching at Holy Cross Catholic School in Bay Settlement. Their mission also included ministering to the people of the parish and serving the poor.[2] The community developed over a number of years and received approval of the first Constitutions from Green Bay's Bishop Francis Xavier Krautbauer on March 14, 1881. At this point, they became a religious order.

Shortly after Sister Madeleine's departure from the chapel on October 24, 1902, Bishop Messmer and Father Fox visited the Superior at St. Francis Convent in Bay Settlement. Their goal was to discuss whether the community would be willing to take over the work at the chapel and to examine how that might transpire. The bishop estimated that, for the time being, one sister would be adequate. St. Francis Convent's Superior, Mother Francis, agreed to send Sister Pauline, who was then stationed at a parish in Delwiche, Wisconsin. Sister Pauline wrote about her arrival in her diary:

> I left my loved Mission to come to the chapel October 28, 1902. Sweet will of God be forever praised. I found two Sisters, twenty children, and forty-two cents. Bishop Messmer, bishop of Green Bay, sent the Bay Settlement Sisters to the chapel to continue the work of instruction especially for the children of the poor.[3]

Heroism of Sister Pauline

With the cupboards bare, twenty hungry children to feed, and only forty-two cents with which to buy food and necessities, Sister Pauline saw the wisdom of God in asking her to leave the work she loved to come help in this desperate situation. Courageously trusting in Divine Providence, Sister Pauline made a trip to Delwiche and appealed to the people there with whom she shared a mutual affection. She solicited funds from them, explaining the severity of the need, and they were generous. However, with no consistent revenue coming in, it was not long before cash and resources were depleted, and Sister Pauline was again left in a desperate situation. In a diary entry on November 15, 1902, she said:

> We were out of bread and I sent the children into the chapel to tell our dear Mother that we were in need of bread. When our prayers were ended, there came a letter from our good Bishop and twenty-five dollars. All I could say was, "God bless and keep him." From that time on we never wanted for anything.[4]

Providing food and clothing for the children and sisters was not the only dilemma Sister Pauline faced. The former administration had left outstanding debts for which Sister Pauline now had to assume responsibility. Again, she went about soliciting funds by setting up special collections at various parishes in the area and asking for donations from other sources as well. Almost miraculously, she was able to completely liquidate a debt of more than a thousand dollars within a year. In her diary, she notes the last payment with the simple words, "*Deo Gratias.*"[5] Soon more sisters and supplies were sent from the Mother House at Bay Settlement to help carry on the work as requested by the bishop. The last two sisters of Adele's group, Sr. Celina Londo and Sr.

Cecilia Frisque, entered the novitiate at Bay Settlement in August, 1903. After taking vows as Sisters of St. Francis of the Holy Cross, they returned to the chapel where they had already given so many years of dedicated service.

Sister Pauline was an extraordinary woman of great holiness and deep faith. She was friendly, well-liked, and demonstrated an exceptional love for God and her neighbor, in whom she saw Christ, especially in the poor. Through the frugality and ingenuity of Sister Pauline and her companions, tuition and board remained exceptionally low. Even more surprising is the fact that most of the boarders were charity cases. To serve them all, it was necessary to initiate annual begging tours that covered the span of miles across the peninsula. Although there was some income from tuition and board, donations were the chief means of support for the institution. Additionally, the sisters depended on donations for the upkeep and improvement of the buildings and grounds around them. Both Bishop Messmer and his successor, Bishop Joseph J. Fox, sent occasional donations for much needed repairs.

A New Era in the Shrine's History

The appointment of Father Smits as pastor of St. Joseph's Catholic Church and chaplain of the chapel marked a new era in its history. He held this position for forty-two years, serving the community and the institution and advising those in charge. Sister Pauline spent eighteen of those years under his wise guiding influence, and from her Father Smits learned the history and traditions of the settlement's past, recording the historical facts and preserving them for future generations. A few weeks after her eightieth birthday, Sister Pauline suffered a paralytic stroke. She died a week later, on March 15, 1926, and was buried in the Convent Cemetery at Bay Settlement next to Sister Pius and Sister Christine, with whom she formed the core of the community of the Sisters of St. Francis at Bay Settlement.[6]

Things continued much the same at the chapel for the next two years. In 1928, however, the Guardian Angel School was opened in Oneida, Wisconsin. Although the chapel school was in good condition, it was no longer up to date, and Bishop Paul P. Rhode decided to close it in favor of the new school. Some of the sisters remained at the chapel at the bishop's request, but in 1933, after a period of consultation, the bishop announced that the school would be remodeled as a Home for Crippled Children. Among various improvements, an elevator was installed. The State Board of Control licensed the Home to act as a child welfare agency and granted a license on June 6, 1933, which stipulated that the number of children there would be limited to twenty.[7]

The sisters worked hard to form a welcoming and joyful home for the children, and each child received care and attention tailored to his or her specific needs. Their devotion to the children attracted attention, and several civic and religious organizations, as well as concerned individuals, took an interest in providing for the advancement and welfare of the children. The sisters were successful in their efforts to create a true home for God's little ones, and the children loved it.

Sr. Jeanne Jarvis was one of the teachers at the Home for Crippled Children and describes it as being like one big, happy family. In the process of serving there, she experienced the transformation of her own spiritual life:

> The people who came there [to visit the chapel] had such a deep faith. I wasn't ready for that. At first, I didn't visit the chapel much because my devotion was more to Jesus than Mary, but then it became one of my favorite places. I grew very much in prayer and seeing all those people come from early in the morning and until late at night

changed me.[8]

Along with this, another change took place. Because Bishop Rhode considered the Home a work of charity, he requested that the compensation the sisters received for their work be recorded as an allowance. Although the allowance was too small to be considered a salary, the bishop canceled all begging tours, and assured the sisters that he would supply the funds whenever financial help was needed.

The Fourth Chapel

Sr. Mary Urban Schumacher served at the chapel from roughly 1960 to 1967. She admits that miracles have taken place at the shrine, but she says there is an even greater miracle taking place there. "So many people come there to ask for prayers. They constantly keep coming because they're drawn there. There are miracles, but the real miracle is the faith of the people and the goodness of those who helped us carry on our ministry there."[9]

For a third time, the number of visitors and patrons outgrew the size of the chapel. Efforts had been underway for many years to gather enough funding for a new one, but without success. There was no hope of building anytime soon. Still, Father Smits was convinced of the need and optimistic about the prospects, and so he told the bishop that if people saw evidence of a building program being put into effect, contributions would begin coming in. Our Lady would see that the contributions would be adequate, he assured him.

The Queen of Heaven kept her word. Bishop Rhode set the building plans in motion, entrusting their supervision to Father Smits. The cornerstone was laid on December 8, 1941, and the new chapel was dedicated by him on July 12, 1942. This red brick chapel was built in Tudor-Gothic style and sized to accommodate three hundred people. As Father Smits had predicted, the contributions continued to flow, and many subsequent, substantial gifts were made in the line of equipment, both for the Children's Home and the Chapel. "In fact, I never worried about the added expense. I felt confident that Our Lady would provide for her shrine, and she did," said Father Smits.[10]

Reevaluation God's Will

During the summer of 1953, diocesan authorities announced that the use of the building as a Home for Crippled Children would be discontinued. State institutions were taking over the work of caring for disabled children. With their broader scope of resources, these agencies were more adept in this field than the sisters were at the time.[11] The home had served its purpose.

After having carried on Sister Adele's mission of instructing children there for more than fifty years, it was time for the Sisters of St. Francis at Bay Settlement to reevaluate God's will for them. The 1950s had seen an influx of vocations to their community, and the sisters needed a larger space to conduct their novitiate. After petitioning the bishop, they were granted use of the chapel school as a pre-novitiate high school for girls aspiring to enter the congregation. The school and convent buildings were rented to the sisters for one dollar per year.[12] They saw this as the continuation of the spirit of Adele's mission. The chapel school would be established as an auxiliary training center that would be used to prepare their young members for their future role as educators, particularly in religious education. It appeared that the Queen of Heaven had granted her approval to this endeavor. With increasingly larger entering classes, the work of instruction continued.[13]

Sister of St. Francis Joanne Goessl started at the pre-novitiate high school when she was fourteen years old. "We live in Adele's spirit," she said. "The message of Mary [during the apparition] is part of our history and in retrospect we see that it has always been a part of our very being. We took to heart Adele's words before she died, 'Be kind to the sick and elderly and continue to instruct the children in their religion.'"[14]

The sisters were blessed with increasing numbers of vocations, and in 1957, a new dormitory was completed to house the young women attending high school classes and religious formation. The tempestuous and rebellious times of the 1960s took a toll, however, not only on society at large, but also on vocations to the religious life. By 1968, there had been a severe decrease in the number of young women wishing to become aspirants and, sadly, the high school was closed. Three sisters remained at the chapel to minister to the pilgrim groups that came. They hired two local women to cook for the groups, and the sisters were paid for use of the facilities.

House of Prayer

In 1972, the former school and convent was transformed into the House of Prayer where the faithful were welcomed for personal retreats, and prayer and Scripture groups conducted by the sisters. They also worked with groups of young people from the area. Beginning in 1973, religious education groups were conducted at the House of Prayer for the neighboring parishes, and full retreats were added to the list of ministries offered. During this time, sisters who taught at the schools in the area resided at the chapel convent, and many varied groups such as the Norbertine Council, Trinity Lutheran Council and Committee, Franciscan Fathers, Franciscan novices, and Boy Scouts made use of the chapel facilities. Area priests also used the buildings and grounds for their parish youth groups. The House of Prayer was further expanded in 1981, and the number of sisters ministering there was increased to five.

Sr. Nancy Langlois resided and helped at the chapel during the 1980s. Time and again, she witnessed the minds and hearts of the people change when they came to pray there. This, in turn, enriched her own faith. She explained that it was common for young people to go there to pray before going out on a date, or for businessmen to go there to pray for the success of their businesses or before making important decisions. During times of crisis, it was natural for people to gather there to beg Mary's intercessory help. Indeed, there was an abundance of both physical and spiritual miracles. However, she believes that one thing is still lacking when considering the mission of the shrine. "Sometimes I think the emphasis is wrong. The chapel is about peace and there needs to be an emphasis on praying for the conversion of sinners as Mary requested during the apparition," she said. She is confident that Our Lady will provide the means for the fulfillment of this request as the chapel's mission continues to unfold.

The Sisters of St. Francis Depart

Despite the fervency of their desire to continue serving the spiritual needs of the people, rising costs and diminishing resources caused the Sisters of St. Francis to reevaluate their work and its future at the chapel. In 1988, they formed a think tank committee of sisters, priests, and laypeople to research future possibilities for the House of Prayer, and submitted their recommendations to the Executive Body of the Sisters of St. Francis the following year. Formal discussions were begun with Green Bay Bishop Adam Maida and other diocesan personnel. On December 9 of that year, the entire community of the Sisters of St. Francis met for a day of discernment at the motherhouse in Green Bay. The result of their discernment was the decision to "discontinue the ministry at the Chapel House of Prayer and dispose of the property." On February 26, Bishop Maida ratified the decision, and on August 31, 1990, the ministry of the Sisters of St. Francis of the Holy Cross at the Chapel of Our Lady of Good Help ended permanently.

A huge debt of gratitude is owed to the Sisters of St. Francis of the Holy Cross who courageously took up Sister Adele's mission after her death. For nearly ninety years, they served selflessly, making great sacrifices for those under their care, and remained faithful to the charism given to them by their founder, Fr. Edward Daems. An April 19, 2019, article in the Green Bay diocesan newspaper paid tribute to the 160-year legacy of the Sisters of St. Francis of the Holy Cross and their almost century-long service at the Chapel of Our Lady of Good Help:

> The ministry of the Sisters of St. Francis of the Holy Cross continues today with sisters serving throughout the Green Bay diocesan community as parish leaders, educators, health caregivers, campus ministers, artists, minority and environmental advocates, social workers, literacy counselors, retreat directors, missionaries, and administrators.[15]

Formal Church Investigation Opens

After the term of the Sisters of St. Francis of the Holy Cross, a brief series of other groups accepted administration of the shrine and grounds. In 2009, Bishop David Ricken opened a formal Church investigation of the apparitions and appointed a commission for the task. Based on the conclusion of the commission, Bishop Ricken approved the 1859 apparitions, and in a formal declaration on December 8, 2010, he stated that they exhibit the substance of supernatural character and are considered worthy of belief. Bishop Ricken also officially recognized the Shrine of Our Lady of Good Help as a diocesan shrine.[16] Since that time, a number of improvements have been made to the property to accommodate the hundreds of thousands of pilgrims that come there each year — among them a large parking lot to better accommodate the volumes of cars and busses, and the Mother of Mercy Hall, a 14,000-square-foot building that seats 1,200 people and was dedicated by Bishop Ricken on April 28, 2019, as part of the 160th anniversary celebration of the apparition.[17]

Regardless of who has been responsible for the property since the first chapel was built in 1861 by Adele's father, Lambert Brise, there has always been a pervading aura of peace there. This feeling of utter peacefulness has been witnessed by innumerable people who have worked at or visited the chapel throughout the more than 160 years of its existence. Perhaps this is why locals have been reticent to share their "secret" of the miraculous happenings that began there in 1859. Who would wish that gift of peace to be disturbed?

"The apparition is in the DNA of the blood that soaks the ground of the land," said Diocese of Green Bay Vicar for Canonical Services Fr. John Girotti. "It's part of the roots of the Belgian ethnic community and preserving the integrity of that heritage is an awesome and grave responsibility."[18]

Chapter Thirteen

WHAT DOES THIS MEAN FOR US?

The number twelve can be found 187 times in the Bible. There are twelve tribes of Israel, twelve patriarchs from Shem to Jacob, and twelve spies spotted the Promised Land. Jesus healed a woman who had been bleeding for twelve years while on his way to raise to life a twelve-year-old girl. He chose twelve apostles, giving them authority to found his Church, administer the sacraments, and to go out to all the nations giving witness to the Good News wherever they went. There are twelve fruits of the Holy Spirit. In biblical times, the number twelve symbolized perfection and authority.[1]

Perhaps this lends some significance to the fact that the Peshtigo Fire took place twelve years, almost to the day, after the apparitions of the Queen of Heaven to Adele Brise. Adele had passionately embraced her mission: to teach the children their catechism, receive the sacraments often, and pray for the conversion of sinners. Our Lady had warned that, if the people did not convert and do penance, her Son would be obliged to punish them. Although Adele carried out her mission dutifully, there were many who did not heed Our Lady's warning. Given that, one could wonder whether the Great Fire was a form of admonition and chastisement, meant not only for the people of that time, but also for future generations.

The apparition at Champion is not the only time Mary has given these instructions and issued such a warning. In most, if not all, of her apparitions over the centuries and throughout the world, she has requested increased devotion, penance, and reparation for the sins of mankind. How sad it must make Our Blessed Mother to see her children ignore her urgent pleading!

Comparing Apparitions

In 1846, Our Lady appeared to two children in La Salette, France. Her messages were poignant, pleading for conversion and warning of the coming famine if the hearts of the people did not change:

> Come to me, my children. Do not be afraid. I am here to tell you something of the greatest importance. If my people will not obey, I shall be compelled to loose my Son's arm. It is so heavy, so pressing that I can no longer restrain it.
>
> How long I have suffered for you! If my Son is not to cast you off, I am obliged to entreat Him without ceasing. But you take no least notice of that. No matter how well you pray in future, no matter how well you act, you will never be able to make up to me what I have endured for

your sake.

"I have appointed for you six days for working. The seventh I have reserved for myself. And no one will give it to me." This is what causes the weight of my Son's arm to be so crushing.

The cart drivers cannot swear without bringing in my Son's name. These are two things that make my Son's arm so burdensome. If the harvest is spoiled it is your fault. I warned you last year (1845) by means of the potatoes.[2] You paid no heed. Quite the reverse, when you discovered that the potatoes had rotted, you swore, you abused my Son's name. They will continue to rot and by Christmas this year there will be none left.

If you have grain, it will do you no good to sow it, for what you sow the beasts will devour, and any part of it that springs up will crumble into dust when you thresh it. A great famine is coming. But before that happens, the children under seven years of age will be seized with trembling and die in their parents' arms. The grownups will pay for their sins by hunger. The grapes will rot and the walnuts will turn bad.

If people are converted, the rocks will become piles of wheat, and it will be found that the potatoes have sown themselves.[3]

Our Lady again issued her urgent request to St. Bernadette Soubirous at Lourdes in 1858:

Penance! Penance! Penance! Pray to God for sinners.

> Go, kiss the ground for the conversion of sinners.
> Go and tell the priests to have a chapel built here.[4]

At the foot of the stone hillside grotto in which she appeared, Mary caused a spring of healing water to burst forth from the dirt. To this day, the spring continues to flow, and the grotto has become one of the world's most popular Catholic pilgrimage places.[5]

In 1917, Mary revealed herself as the Lady of the Rosary to three shepherd children at Fátima, Portugal. She told them:

> I am the Lady of the Rosary, I have come to warn the faithful to amend their lives and ask for pardon for their sins. They must not offend Our Lord any more, for He is already too grievously offended by the sins of men. People must say the Rosary. Let them continue saying it every day.[6]

In the village of Kibeho, Rwanda, Our Lady appeared to three high school girls from 1982 to 1989. Five years later, the Rwandan genocide began, claiming the lives of more than 800,000 people and devastating the country.[7]

> When I show myself to someone and talk to them, I want to turn to the whole world. If I am turning to the parish of Kibeho, it does not mean that I am concerned only for Kibeho or for the Diocese of Butare or for Rwanda, or for the whole of Africa. I am concerned with and turning to the whole world. The world is evil and rushes towards its ruin. It is about to fall in its abyss. The world is in rebellion against God. Many sins are being committed. There is no love and no peace. If you do not repent and convert your hearts, you will all fall into an abyss.[8]

Author and Marian theologian Fr. Edward Looney compares Our Lady of Good Help with other well-known apparitions:

> Champion is consonant with many of Mary's other apparitions. In Guadalupe, the Virgin appeared to an adult man, just as Adele was an adult woman. Both Juan Diego and Adele became missionaries after the reception of their apparitions. In Champion, Mary identified her heavenly mission of praying for the conversion of sinners. In La Salette, conversion was needed so people would obey the commandments. In Lourdes, Mary spoke about penance, and in Champion she requested penance to prevent punishment from God. In Fátima, Our Lady requested reparation for sins — the next step beyond personal penance. A year before in Lourdes, Mary said she is the Immaculate Conception and in Champion the Queen of Heaven — the beginning and end of her life. St. Bernadette had Mary for a catechist for her first Holy Communion whereas Adele prepared students for their first Holy Communion. Many parallels can be drawn. In the end, the messages are so similar: pray, convert, and do penance. These are messages from a mother who loves her children and wants what is best for us — life with God in the Kingdom of Heaven.[9]

A Message for Today's "Wild Country"

It seems, then, that the apparitions of Mary at Champion were meant not only for the 1859 wild country of northeastern Wisconsin, but for the entire United States, and the whole world beyond the limits of time. Mary's appearance as Queen of Heaven to Adele Brise was not happenstance, but rather a calculated act of love and mercy. Her warning is stern and yet filled with ardor and concern for her children. She wants to envelope us in her

Immaculate Heart so that we spend eternity with her in heaven. That she appeared with such a message here in our own country is not a coincidence and should not be taken lightly. In a sense, the faithful of the United States have become the custodians of the message and mission of Champion. The Mother of God has given this to us. As such, it is our responsibility to understand, internalize, and embrace it.

According to Michael O'Neill:

> Many major Church-approved apparitions — Fátima for example — have messages and meaning that are intended for the entire world. The apparitions at Champion perhaps have, at least initially, had a more decidedly local focus. Although the mission given to Adele to catechize the young is tied to apparitions and the local surroundings from over a century and a half ago, that need to teach the faith to a new generation of children is as great as it ever was in the history of Christianity.

He continues:

> Church doctrine and dogma are being rejected and ignored in current times as part of society's large-scale rebellion against organized religion — but this does not change the innate hunger of both believers and non-believers alike for the supernatural. People are naturally curious and inspired by stories of miracles and the accounts of a Church-validated Marian apparition paired with the claims of modern medical healings happening in America will continue to inspire the fascination and faith of people for many years to come.[10]

In examining the story of Our Lady of Good Help, we must not only look backwards in order to learn from it; we must look forward to secure its continual implementation. As Green Bay Bishop David L. Ricken stated:

> Our Blessed Mother instructed Adele to "*teach the children of this wild country what they need to know for salvation.*" We believe very strongly in this message for today. Though Our Blessed Lady gave this message to Adele, it has been made manifestly clear throughout the one-hundred-sixty-year history of this Shrine, that this ministry is timeless and applies to all spiritual children. This "*wild country*" is of course the world of fear and anxiety we all experience; but it is also the wilderness of our souls struggling to navigate the pitfalls of our own sinful inclinations. The message and ministry of the Champion Shrine labors to provide its pilgrims with a pathway to peace. This is needed in our current times seemingly more than ever.[11]

Going Forward

Just as the message of Our Lady at Champion endows the faithful with a great mission, it also imparts a great mission to the Shrine itself. Bishop Ricken said:

> As the National Shrine of Our Lady of Good Help continues to grow and expand its outreach, it is becoming increasingly clear that Our Blessed Mother desires this place to be an oasis of refuge. All who visit step away with an abiding sense of peace and an encounter with God. Instruction on the pathway to salvation, as Our Lady taught, begins with relationship. Pilgrims visit with the intention of learning more of the nature of these apparitions, but they leave with an experience of

the person of Jesus. As the spirit of the world continues to grow and dominate minds and hearts, so the light of Christ shines all the brighter through the intercession and loving guidance of the Blessed Mother of God. The impact of this Shrine and its mission and ministry moving forward will be nothing short of the preservation of the faith in the souls of countless believers.[12]

Going forward, we must ask ourselves two questions: How will we make America's Mary our own? How will we embody the story of Our Lady of Good Help? Our country, our world, is depending on us. It begins with our own conversion — prayer (especially the Rosary), penance, frequent reception of the sacraments, catechesis, fidelity to the Magisterium of the Church, and ardent devotion to Our Lord and his Mother. It endures when we live our faith heroically in every aspect of our lives and confidently share it with others. The duty can feel daunting, but Mary's words to Adele Brise are also her words to us: "Go, and fear nothing. I will help you."

AFTERWORD

By Fr. Edward Looney

You picked up Marge Fenelon's book about America's Mary for a reason. The first and foremost reason is because God wanted you to, and you said yes. Maybe you have been struggling with belief or sin in your life, and Our Lady's words helped you believe more or prompted you to change your life and conform it more to the Gospel. Or you may have been curious about this apparition and wanted to know more. You might be visiting Wisconsin, whether with religious or secular motivation, and thought you might want to visit the shrine in Champion. By reading this story and history, you are now familiar with Adele Brise and Mary's message. Now it's time to make your pilgrimage.

I've traveled to Marian shrines throughout the United States and the world. And I've visited Champion more times than I can count. The one thing I have consistently observed is that pilgrims don't know what to do when they are there. Sometimes individuals don't understand what is so special about the place, and they also might miss some of the important things at the Shrine. I'm glad you know why Champion is so special. What should you do when you visit?

First, go to confession either before or during your pilgrimage. Confessions are heard daily at the shrine. Our Lady told Adele to make a general confession. You might not need to do that right now, but confession was important to Our Lady for Adele, and now as we follow in her footsteps, it should be for us as well.

Second, attend Mass and receive holy Communion. Our Lady told Adele to offer her holy Communion for the conversion of sinners. After you receive Our Lord, go back to the pew, kneel down, and say a prayer similar to this:

> Jesus, thank you for allowing me to receive you today. I offer my holy Communion to you, and beg from you the conversion of sinners, beginning with me, my family, my friends, those I love, and the entire world. Reveal yourself to them so that they may know your love and soon receive your love in holy Communion.

Praying a prayer like this continues to fulfill Our Lady's request to Adele to this very day.

Third, visit the Apparition Oratory. This is where pilgrims have prayed for decades and have lit their candles. It's a place where miracles and healings have happened. As you visit Champion, I hope you will pray a Rosary. The oratory is a good place to do that. So often, I see pilgrims visit the sacred spot at any shrine for a few moments. Spend some quality time with Our

Lady. Kneel before her statue and reflect on the love the Queen of Heaven has for you. Also while in the oratory, this would be a good place to remember all the people for whom you want to pray, all of the petitions that you carry in your heart.

Fourth, explore the property. Walk the Rosary path and visit the Stations of the Cross and the various grottos. As you do so, remember where you are walking was spared the night of the fire in October 1871.

Fifth, visit the welcome center (maybe you should do that first). There will be information for you to see, allowing you to continue to learn or refresh your memory about the facts of the Shrine.

You may wish to pray nine days before or after your pilgrimage. This is a novena. It will ready your heart and mind for your pilgrimage experience.

If you haven't visited Champion, I hope you will be able to soon. If you are a returning pilgrim, welcome back to Mary's home. And if you can't afford a pilgrimage or are unable to do so for some other reason, make a spiritual pilgrimage. Participate as much as you can via virtual means. And in the spirit of Saint Faustina, send your guardian angel to the Shrine with your petitions.

Whether you are at the shrine or at your home, Our Lady wants to help you just as she did in Adele's life and over the years in the lives of pilgrims. Her help is available to all of us, no matter where we are, whenever we ask her to pray for us.

PRAYER TO OUR LADY OF GOOD HELP

ODear Lady of Good Help, you revealed yourself as the Queen of Heaven to your servant Adele. You gave her a mission to pray for the conversion of sinners, to bring the Good News of Jesus Christ to others and to prepare the children for the reception of the sacraments.

I trust that as you called Adele to holiness, you are calling me, in my station in life, to live a holy life, devoted to Jesus Christ with the help of your maternal love.

I bring before you now my worries and anxieties. I abandon my attachments to them and place them at your feet.

I ask you to hear the deepest longings of my heart as I pray most earnestly for: _____ (your intention).

Dear Lady, you told Adele and you say to all of us, "Do not be afraid; I will help you." Help me now as I place this intention with complete confidence and trust.

Our Father … ; Hail Mary … ; Glory Be …

Our Lady of Good Help, pray for us.

Official prayer composed by Most Reverend David L. Ricken, D.D., J.C.L., Bishop of the Diocese of Green Bay

ACKNOWLEDGMENTS

This book would not have been possible without the gracious support of Bishop David L. Ricken, Fr. John Girotti, the Archives staff, and so many others of the Diocese of Green Bay. Equally so was the help and support I received from the Shrine of Our Lady of Good Help staff, particularly former director of communications Corrie Campbell and Rector Fr. John Broussard, as well as the time given to me by locals Joan Dalebroux and Patricia Boerschinger. I'm grateful to the Sisters of St. Francis of the Holy Cross (known in the manuscript as Bay Settlement Sisters) for opening their home and heart to me, and granting me interviews and access to their archives. Special thanks to Sr. Nancy Langlois for gifting me with one of the original devotional booklets ever printed and dedicated to Sr. Adele Brise. It is a precious gift I will always cherish. My husband (#herohusband) gave selflessly of himself to allot me time and energy to work on the book, accompanying me on research trips to the shrine, praying with me, and cheering me on throughout the barrage of obstacles and challenges along the way. Finally, I owe this book to the editorial and creative staff at Our Sunday Visitor, beginning with Sarah Reinhard and down the list. The person most deserving of credit is my editor, Mary Beth Giltner, for her prayers, patient understanding, creative problem-solving, and unwavering belief in me over the past three years. Ultimately, I must thank Sister Adele for her companionship and ever-present intercession for me at the throne of the Queen of Heaven.

TIMELINE

*Used with permission, National Shrine
of Our Lady of Good Help*

1831   January 30, Marie Adele Joseph Brise is born
        at Dion-le-Val, Belgium.

1855   August 7, Lambert and Marie Brise purchase
        two hundred and forty acres of land in the
        town of Red River, Wisconsin.

1859   October 9, apparition of the Virgin Mary to
        Adele Brise. Small oratory built of logs the
        same year.

1861   Second chapel — a frame structure built at
        the Shrine.

1865–   Between these dates, a frame convent and
1868   school are built near the Chapel.

1869   School is formally announced as St. Mary's
        Academy.

1871   October 8, the Great Fires of Northern
        Wisconsin, popularly known as the Peshtigo
        Fire, rage.

1880   The third chapel, a brick structure, is built.

1885   The brick convent and school are built. Joseph
        Renè Vilatte establishes himself in the center
        of a Catholic community on the Door
        Peninsula.

1890   Death of Sister "Maggie" (Marguerite Allard),
        Tertiary at the Chapel.

1893   Two Praemonstratensian (Norbertine) Fathers
        and one lay brother arrive from Berne Abbey
        in Holland to labor among the Catholics of
        Door Peninsula.

1896   July 5, Sr. Adele Brise dies at the chapel.

1902   October, the Most Rev. Sebastian Messmer,
        D.D., bishop of Green Bay, entrusts the work
        at the chapel to the Sisters of St. Francis from
        Bay Settlement.

1926   March 15, Sister Pauline dies at the chapel at
        the age of eighty.

1933   The brick convent and school are remodeled
        as a Home for Crippled Children.

1941   December 8, the Most Rev. Paul P. Rhode,
        bishop of Green Bay, lays the cornerstone for
        the fourth chapel.

1942   July 12, the new chapel is dedicated by Bishop

Rhode under the title "Our Lady of Good
Help."

1953   Summer, the chapel school is converted into
a pre-novitiate for the Sisters of St. Francis
whose Mother House is at Bay Settlement.
(The current Mother House is located in
Green Bay, Wisconsin.)

1954   Most Rev. S. V. Bona is appointed the first
resident chaplain for the chapel.

1956   Because of the increase in vocations, a new
dormitory is built on the chapel grounds to
house the young women attending high
school and religious formation.

1968   The Franciscan pre-novitiate high school is
closed due to lack of vocations. The
Franciscan Sisters continue on at the chapel
serving the people in the area. Three
Benedictine priests arrive at the chapel.

1969   Benedictine priests leave the chapel.

1992   The Shrine is entrusted to nine Carmelite
Sisters from Grand Rapids, Michigan, and the
Monastery of the Holy Name of Jesus is
founded.

2002   Bishop David L. Ricken of Green Bay opens a
formal Church investigation of the apparitions
that occurred on the site in 1859 and appoints

a commission for the task.

2010   December 8, Bishop Ricken issues a formal declaration approving the 1859 apparitions and states that they exhibit the substance of supernatural character and are considered worthy of belief. Bishop Ricken also officially recognizes the Shrine of Our Lady of Good Help as a Diocesan Shrine.

2011   July 7, Fathers of Mercy (order based in Auburn, Kentucky) assume the rectorship and chaplaincy of the shrine.

NOTES

Chapter One: APPARITION OR IMAGINATION?

1. William Thomas Walsh, *Our Lady of Fatima* (London: The Macmillan Company, 1949), 58.

2. Walsh, *Our Lady of Fatima*, 112.

3. Charles J. Scicluna, "Doctrinal Guidelines and Competencies of the Diocesan Bishop and the Congregations for the Doctrine of the Faith in the Discernment of the Marian Apparition," The Miracle Hunter, http://www.miraclehunter.com/marian_apparitions /discernment/scicluna.html.

4. Peter Joseph, "Apparitions True and False," The Miracle Hunter, http://miraclehunter.com/marian_apparitions/discernment /fr_peter_joseph.html.

5. Michael O'Neill, "The Discernment of Miracle Claims," The Miracle Hunter, http://www.miraclehunter.com/marian_apparitions /discernment/.

6. The Council of Trent, "The canons and decrees of the sacred and OEcumenical Council of Trent," ed. and trans. J. Waterworth (London: Dolman, 1848), Session the Twenty-Fifth, https://history .hanover.edu/texts/trent/trentall.html.

7. O'Neill, "The Discernment of Miracle Claims."

8. Benedict XVI, *Verbum Domini*, Vatican.va, par. 14.

9. The Canon Law Society of America, *New Commentary on the Code of Canon Law*, ed. by John P. Beal, James A. Coriden, and Thomas J. Green (New York: Paulist Press, 2000), Canon 212.

10. The Canon Law Society of America, Canon 753, 918.

11. John Girotti, Vicar for Canonical Services for the Diocese of Green Bay, in conversation with the author, July 2018.

12. David L. Ricken, Bishop of Green Bay, in conversation with the author, July 2018.

13. Ricken, in conversation with the author, July 2018.

14. Dominica Shallow, OSF, *The Shrine of Our Lady of Good Help: A History* (The Shrine of Our Lady of Good Help, 2014), 5.

Chapter Two: BELGIAN EMIGRATION TO AMERICA

1. Hjalmar Rued Holand, *Wisconsin's Belgian Community: An Account of the Early Events in the Belgian Settlement of Northeastern Wisconsin with Particular Reference to the Belgians in Door County* (Sturgeon Bay, Wisconsin: Door County Historical Society, 1933), 1.

2. Holand, *Wisconsin's Belgian Community*, 10.

3. "History of Belgian Settlement Is Part of Tlachac's Legacy," *Algoma Record-Herald*, vol. 101, no. 4, June 27, 1973, 2.

4. Ibid.

5. The Belgian hektari equals approximately one and one-fourth American acres. *Algoma Record-Herald*, vol. 101, no. 4, 1.

6. Holand, *Wisconsin's Belgian Community*, 11.

7. *Algoma Record-Herald*, 2.

8. Ibid.

9. Ibid.

10. CPI Inflations Calculator, https://www.officialdata.org/us/inflation/1835?amount=35.

11. Holand, *Wisconsin's Belgian Community*, 12.

12. *Algoma Record-Herald*, vol. 101, no. 6, 3.

13. Ibid., 12.

14. Ibid.

15. Ibid.

16. Ibid.

17. Ibid.

18. Sheboygan County Wisconsin, "A History of Sheboygan County," https://www.sheboygancounty.com/government/about-the-county/history.

19. Holand, *Wisconsin's Belgian Community*, 13.

20. Ibid.

21. Ibid., 14.

Chapter Three: THE METTLE OF THE BELGIAN PEOPLE

1. Roy and Charlotte Lukes, "Old-Growth Forests," *Door County Pulse*, September 6, 2010, https://doorcountypulse.com/old-growth -forests/.

2. Wisconsin County Forests Association, https://www .wisconsincountyforests.com/education/trees-of-wi/.

3. *Algoma Record-Herald*, "History of Belgian Settlement Is Part of Tlachac's Legacy," vol. 101, no. 3, 2.

4. Members of the Potawatomi Tribe according to *Algoma Record-Herald*, vol. 101, no. 3, 6.

5. Shallow, *The Shrine of Our Lady of Good Help*, 16.

6. "History of Belgian Settlement Is Part of Tlachac's Legacy," *Algoma Record-Herald*, vol. 101, no. 3, 2.

7. "Collecting Maple Sugar," Encyclopedia.com.

8. *Algoma Record-Herald*, vol. 101, no. 4, 9.

9. Holand, 15.

10. *Algoma Record-Herald*, 9.

11. *Algoma Record-Herald*, vol. 101, no. 4, 6.

12. Holand, *Wisconsin's Belgian Community*, 16.

13. Asiatic cholera is a highly contagious and primarily water-borne disease with high fatality rates. Symptoms begin to appear a few hours and up to five days after contact and include severe diarrhea and vomiting, causing rapid dehydration. It is accompanied by fatigue, painful muscle cramps, feeble voice, skin shriveling, bluish to purplish discoloration, and sunken eyes. TheFreeDictionary.com, *The Free Medical Dictionary*, "Asiatic Cholera," https://medical-dictionary .thefreedictionary.com/Asiatic+cholera.

14. Holand, *Wisconsin's Belgian Community*, 16.

15. Peter G. Sanchez, "Understanding the church's teaching on

burying the dead," *Catholic Star Herald*, April 6, 2017, https://
catholicstarherald.org/understanding-the-churchs-teaching-on-burying
-the-dead/.

16. Shallow, *The Shrine of Our Lady of Good Help*, 16.

17. Ibid., 18.

18. It was during the final influx of Belgian immigration that
Adele Brise's family came to Wisconsin. Although it isn't clear on
which ship they traveled, land records show that Lambert Brise,
Adele's father, and his wife, Marie, purchased 240 acres of land in the
town of Red River, Wisconsin, in 1855.

19. Hjalmar R. Holand, M.A., "History of the Belgian Settlement,
Door County, Wisconsin" in *History of Door County, Wisconsin The
County Beautiful* (S.J. Clark Publishing Company, 1917), https://
books.google.com/books?id=4Fo0AQAAMAAJ.

20. *Algoma Record-Herald*, 9.

21. A cutting tool with handle and blade at right angles. Dictio-
nary.com, https://www.dictionary.com/browse/froe.

22. Shakes are a defined lengthwise separation of the wood along
the grain, usually occurring between or through the rings of annual
growth. Southern Pine Inspection Bureau, "Shakes, Checks, and Splits
in Dimension Lumber", https://blog.spib.org/shakes-checks-and
-splits-in-dimension-lumber/.

23. A draw knife consists of a long blade that tapers on either
side. One edge tapers down into a bevel, which is drawn over the
wood surface. Hence, the name "draw knife." The other side of the
blade extends into two tangs to which the handles are attached at a
right angle to the blade. These two handles on either side make a draw
knife look similar to the handlebars of a bicycle. The Art of Hand
Tools, "What is the Difference Between a Spokeshave and a Draw
Knife?", https://theartofhandtools.com/what-is-the-difference-between-
a-spokeshave
-and-a-draw-knife/.

24. *Algoma Record-Herald*, vol. 101, number 10, 11.

25. Wisconsin Historical Society, "Wisconsin's Involvement in the Civil War", https://www.wisconsinhistory.org/Records/Article/CS3355.

26. *Algoma Record-Herald*, 11.

Chapter Four: BELGIAN FAITH AND TRADITION

1. Holand, *Wisconsin's Belgian Community*, Introduction.

2. Walloon Belgians of the Door Peninsula, "Walloon Belgians," http://walloonbelgiansdoorpeninsula.weebly.com/walloons.html.

3. Author interview with Corrie Campbell, National Shrine of Our Lady of Good Help Communications and Events Coordinator, June 23, 2017.

4. Belgian Heritage Center, "Historic Timeline," http://www.belgianheritagecenter.org/en-us/history/default.aspx.

5. Holand, *Wisconsin's Belgian Community*, 22.

6. Ibid.

7. University of Wisconsin — Madison Libraries, *Wallonie en Porte:* Door County Belgians, Chapter 19, p. 79, https://search.library.wisc.edu/digital/A4IDO4FG35TBNZ8A.

8. Holand, *Wisconsin's Belgian Community*, 95.

9. Walloon-Belgians of the Door Peninsula, "Roadside Chapels," http://walloonbelgiansdoorpeninsula.weebly.com/roadside-chapels.html.

10. Author interview with Fr. Edward Looney, March 16, 2021.

Chapter Five: FR. EDWARD DAEMS

1. Louise Hunt, OSF, *A History of the Sisters of St. Francis of the Holy Cross 1868-1995* (Green Bay, Wisconsin: Sisters of St. Francis of the Holy Cross, no date), 9.

2. Crosier Fathers & Brothers, "The Crosiers," https://crosier.org/our-ministry/international/.

3. Hunt, *A History of the Sisters of St. Francis*, 9.

4. Ibid., 10.

5. Ibid.

6. Ibid., 10.

7. Ibid., 11.

8. Holand, *Wisconsin's Belgian Community*, 99.

9. Hunt, *A History of the Sisters of St. Francis*, 11.

10. Ibid., 12.

11. Ibid.

12. Ibid.

13. Ibid.

14. "Trusteeism, in Roman Catholicism, a controversy concerning lay control of parish administration in the late 18th and 19th centuries in the United States. Several state legislatures had recognized elected lay representatives (trustees) as the legal administrators of parishes. Although church law did not forbid lay participation in some aspects of church life, it was emphatic concerning the bishop's prerogative of appointing and dismissing the pastors of parishes. Crises thus arose when trustees invoked civil law to dismiss unpopular pastors, sometimes because they were from different ethnic backgrounds than their parishioners." "Trusteeism," Britannica.com.

15. Shallow, *The Shrine of Our Lady of Good Help*, 35.

16. Ibid.

17. Holand, *Wisconsin's Belgian Community*, 100.

Chapter Six: ADELE BRISE AND HER FAMILY

1. "Brief History of the Apparitions of Our Lady of Kibeho," Kibeho-Cana.org, https://www.kibeho-cana.org/a-brief-history-of-the-apparitions-of-our-lady-of-kibeho/.

2. "Fátima Apparitions," TheHolyRosary.org, https://www.theholyrosary.org/fatimaapparitions.

3. "La Salette, France (1846)," The Miracle Hunter, http://miraclehunter.com/marian_apparitions/approved_apparitions/lasalette

/index.html.

4. "St. Bernadette of Lourdes," Britannica.com, https://www
.britannica.com/biography/Saint-Bernadette-of-Lourdes.

5. Edward Looney, (2011) "Called to Evangelize: The Story of
Adele Brise and the Mariophany that Changed Her Life," *Marian
Studies* vol. 62, Article 10, https://ecommons.udayton.edu/marian
_studies/vol62/iss1/10.

6. Shallow, *The Shrine of Our Lady of Good Help*, 17.

7. Ibid.

8. Holand, *Wisconsin's Belgian Community*, 38.

9. Author interview with Corrie Campbell, National Shrine of
Our Lady of Good Help Communications Director, June 23, 2017.

10. *Adele Brise* (Green Bay, Archives of the Sisters of St. Francis
of the Holy Cross, circa 1909), 7.

11. Peter Pernin, *The Finger of God is There*, Appendix (Montre-
al, Lovell, 1874), 95.

Chapter Seven: THE APPARITIONS

1. National Shrine of Our Lady of Good Help historians believe
the grist mill Adele walked to was in Dykesville, Wisconsin — approximately four to six miles away. Author interview with Corrie Campbell, Communications Director, July 17, 2018.

2. Sister Pauline expressed some doubt as to the exact year in
which the apparitions took place. She thought perhaps they had
occurred in 1857, and a priest familiar with the case, Father DeKelver,
believed it was 1858. However, matching years with the days of the
week and the various accounts would place the apparitions in 1859,
and other records have verified this.

3. Rev. William Verhoeff, OSC, pastor of Holy Cross Church at
Bay Settlement at the time of the apparitions.

4. Shallow, *The Shrine of Our Lady of Good Help*, 19–22.

5. Shallow, *The Shrine of Our Lady of Good Help*.

6. This account appears in a ledger of copies of letters that were

recorded by Sister Adele's secretary. The handwriting in the original is that of the secretary and not Adele, nor was it her signature. It is believed that Sister Adele dictated the letters, and two copies were made. One would take the form of a letter that was sent to the addressee, the other was a duplicate recorded in the ledger book. Sister Adele Brise, *Letters by Sr. Adele, 1887-1890*, vol. II, *1887-1890* (Robinsonville, Sisters of Saint Francis of the Holy Cross Bay Settlement Archives), 306.

7. A supernatural appreciation of faith on the part of the whole body of the faithful which cannot err and manifests a universal consent in matters of faith and morals in adherence to the Magisterium. Cf. *Catechism of the Catholic Church*, par. 92.

Chapter Eight: ADELE'S MISSIONARY ZEAL

1. University of Wisconsin-Madison, Wade Institute for German-American Studies, "Ethnic Groups in Wisconsin: Historical Background," https://mki.wisc.edu/ethnic-groups-in-wisconsin-historical-background/.

2. Looney, "Called to Evangelize", Vol. 62, Article 10.

3. Shallow, *The Shrine of Our Lady of Good Help*, 14.

4. Looney, "Called to Evangelize", Vol. 62, Article 10.

5. Shallow, *The Shrine of Our Lady of Good Help*, 22.

6. *Kewaunee Enterprise*, February 22, 1871, as quoted in Shallow, *The Shrine of Our Lady of Good Help*, 22.

7. Ibid.

8. Patricia Kasten, "Did Adele Brise belong to a religious community?" *The Compass*, April 27, 2018, 4A.

9. Looney, "Called to Evangelize", Vol. 62, Article 10.

10. Shallow, *The Shrine of Our Lady of Good Help*, 24.

11. Sisters of St. Francis of the Holy Cross, Chronology, archive photocopy, date unknown.

12. Shallow, *The Shrine of Our Lady of Good Help*, 25.

13. Sisters of St. Francis of Assisi, Chronology.

14. The community of women founded by Adele were referred

to both as the Sisters of Good Help and Sisters of Good Health. Adele referred to them as the Sisters of St. Francis of Assisi, as they were Third Order Secular Franciscans.

15. *Kewaunee Enterprise*, February 22, 1871, as quoted in Shallow, *The Shrine of Our Lady of Good Help*, 26.

16. Ibid., 27.

17. Ibid.

18. Ibid., 27.

19. Josephine Prindaville, *History of Catholic Education in the Diocese of Green Bay* (Oshkosh, Castle-Pierce Printing Co.), 40, as quoted in Shallow, *The Shrine of Our Lady of Good Help*, 28.

20. Shallow, *The Shrine of Our Lady of Good Help*, 28.

21. Ibid.

22. Given the tenderness and devotion of Sister Adele for the children in her charge and her knowledge of the love and mercy of God, it is more likely that this was a symbolic gesture of gratitude and affection for the children's parents and not a ritual of public shaming as it may appear.

23. Diocese of Green Bay Archives, DR-47, Series 7, no date.

24. Ibid.

25. Ibid.

26. The signature on the letter is that of Sr. Marie of the Sacred Heart and cites as location the Monastery of the Precious Blood in Gravelbourg, Saskatchewan, Canada. From this, it could be surmised that Ms. Allard became a religious sister after marrying, having children, and becoming a widow.

27. Diocese of Green Bay Archives, DR-47, Series 7.

28. Diocese of Green Bay Archives, DR-47, Series 7, folder 3.

Chapter Nine: THE GREAT FIRE AND THE GREAT MIRACLE

1. Peshtigo Fire Museum, "The Story of the Peshtigo Fire," Chapter 1, "Before the Fire," http://www.peshtigofiremuseum.com/fire/.

2. Shallow, *The Shrine of Our Lady of Good Help*, 30.

3. Rev. Peter Pernin, *The Great Peshtigo Fire: An Eye Witness Account* (Madison, WI: Wisconsin Historical Society Press, 1999), 16–17.

4. Pernin, *The Great Peshtigo Fire*, 19.

5. Ibid., 24.

6. Ibid., 26.

7. Ibid., 29–30.

8. Ibid., 31–32.

9. Peshtigo Fire Museum, "The Story of the Peshtigo Fire."

10. Shallow, *The Shrine of Our Lady of Good Help*, 31.

11. *State Gazette*, November 13, 1871, as quoted in Shallow, *The Shrine of Our Lady of Good Help*, 32.

12. Ashley Saxe and Corrie Campbell, *The Good News: News and Events from the National Shrine of Our Lady of Good Help*, October–December 2018, Issue #49, 6.

13. Peter Pernin, as quoted in Shallow, *The Shrine of Our Lady of Good Help*, 32–33.

14. Marc Lallanilla, "Whirling Flames: How Fire Tornadoes Work," LiveScience.com, May 16, 2014, https://www.livescience.com/45676-what-is-a-firenado.html.

15. *The Good News*, Issue #49, 6.

Chapter Ten: TRIALS AND PERSECUTION

1. Adele Brise formed the tertiary community under the name "Sisters of St. Francis." However, locals most often referred to them as the Sisters of Good Help.

2. Shallow, *The Shrine of Our Lady of Good Help*, 33.

3. Ibid.

4. Milo P. Smits, O. Praem in an interview with Dominica Shallow, OSF, as quoted in Shallow, *The Shrine of Our Lady of Good Help*, 34. Father Smits obtained this knowledge from Sister Pauline and verified the facts with many of the old pioneers in Bay Settlement.

5. Shallow, *The Shrine of Our Lady of Good Help*.

6. Ibid., 35–36.

7. Letter written to Bishop Krautbauer and signed by Sister Adele and six members of her group, dated July 20, 1875. Diocesan Files, Bishop's House, Green Bay, Wisconsin, as quoted in Shallow, *The Shrine of Our Lady of Good Help*, 36.

8. Letter written.

9. Holand, *Wisconsin's Belgian Community*, 75–76.

10. Ibid., 77.

11. Shallow, *The Shrine of Our Lady of Good Help*, 37.

12. Joseph Marx, and Benjamin Blied, "Old Catholics in America," *The Salesianum* v. 36, 1941, pp. 156–57, as quoted in Shallow, *The Shrine of Our Lady of Good Help*, 37.

13. Shallow, *The Shrine of Our Lady of Good Help*, 38.

14. Ibid.

15. Ibid., 39.

Chapter Eleven: FULFILLING ADELE'S MISSION

1. "The mendicant orders are marked by two characteristics: poverty, practiced in common; and the mixed life, that is the union of contemplation with the work of the sacred ministry. Moreover, the mendicant orders present the appearance of a religious army, the soldiers of which are moved about by their superiors, without being attached to any particular convent, and recognize a hierarchy of local, provincial, and general superiors. The order, or at least the province, takes the place of the monastery. Other important points may be noticed: the mendicant orders are founded only by favor of an express approbation of the sovereign pontiff, who approves their rules or constitutions. They adopt the form of vows which relates explicitly to poverty, chastity, and obedience." *Catholic Answers Encyclopedia*, "Religious Life," https://www.catholic.com/encyclopedia /religious-life.

2. Shallow, *The Shrine of Our Lady of Good Help*, 47–48.

3. R. Greven, "I Am the Queen of Heaven," *The story of the*

Chapel at Robinsonville, Wisconsin (1910), 12-13, as quoted in Shallow, *The Shrine of Our Lady of Good Help*, 44.

4. *Green Bay Advocate*, October 13, 1881, as quoted in Shallow, *The Shrine of Our Lady of Good Help*, 44.

5. The precise location of the tree stumps cannot be absolutely proven, but it is certain that the altar of the current chapel is within close proximity to the place where Mary appeared, and the Apparition Oratory within close proximity of the location of the tree roots. Thus the exact spot on which the apparitions took place cannot be proven either. For this the Church relies on pious tradition and has not made a definitive judgment. Author interview with Fr. John Girotti, Vicar for Canonical Services for the Diocese of Green Bay, July 17, 2018.

6. Patricia Kasten, "Carved, wooden statue of Mary dates back to early 1900s," *The Compass*, April 19, 2019, 9A.

7. Ibid.

8. Ibid.

9. Captain John Denessen (1836–1898) was born in North Brabant, Holland, and came to the United States with his parents at age twelve. His mother died shortly thereafter, and the family lived for a time in Little Chute before moving to Bay Settlement. He became profitable in the boating business, and in the spring of 1882 he built the steamer *John Denessen*. In 1889, he purchased the steamer *Schiller*, which was lengthened and rechristened the *Nettie Denessen*, which he operated until his retirement. It is unclear which of the two steamers are referred to in the text. "Johannes Denessen," FindAGrave.com.

10. Exact date unknown.

11. Patricia Kasten, "Carved, wooden statue of Mary", 12A.

12. The processional statue of Mary is kept in the National Shrine of Our Lady of Good Help Welcome Center.

13. *Kewanee Enterprise*, as quoted in Shallow, *The Shrine of Our Lady of Good Help*, 50.

14. Shallow, *The Shrine of Our Lady of Good Help*, 52.

15. *Green Bay Advocate*, August 1926, as quoted in Shallow, *The*

Shrine of Our Lady of Good Help, 52.

16. Author interview with Patricia Boerschinger, August 21, 2018.

17. Shallow, *The Shrine of Our Lady of Good Help*, 52–53.

18. Author interview with Patricia Boerschinger, August 21, 2018.

19. Philip Kosloski, "This is how miracles are approved by the Church," Aleteia.com, May 14, 2018.

20. Shallow, *The Shrine of Our Lady of Good Help*, 53.

21. Ibid., 54.

22. Diphtheria is a serious bacterial infection that usually affects the mucous membranes of the nose and throat. It can be treated with medications. But in advanced stages, diphtheria can damage the heart, kidneys, and nervous system. Even with treatment, diphtheria can be deadly, especially in children. "Diptheria," MayoClinic.com.

23. In the nineteenth century, disinfectants were used as therapeutics. This small group of medicines was used in the prevention of communicable disease. Research showed that some illnesses were caused by living organisms that were visible only under a microscope. These diseases could be prevented or cured by killing the organism or stopping its growth in the body. The main disinfectants were carbolic, chlorine, lime, charcoal, and sulphur. Melnick Medical Museum, "Medical Treatments in the Late 19th Century," https://melnickmedicalmuseum.com/2013/03/27/19ctreatment/.

24. Adalbert "Vojtech" Cipin, *The Czech Catholic Parishes in Northeastern Wisconsin*, trans. Raymond Selner, (no date), 15.

25. Cipin, *The Czech Catholic Parishes*.

26. Ibid., 54.

27. Author interview with National Shrine of Our Lady of Good Help docent Lisa Larson and Communications Director Corrie Campbell, June 23, 2017.

28. Croup refers to an infection of the upper airway, which obstructs breathing and causes a characteristic barking cough. "Croup,"

MayoClinic.com.

29. Shallow, *The Shrine of Our Lady of Good Help*, 55.

30. R. Greven, as quoted in Shallow, *The Shrine of Our Lady of Good Help*, 66.

31. Shallow, *The Shrine of Our Lady of Good Help*, 56.

Chapter Twelve: SISTERS OF ST. FRANCIS OF THE HOLY CROSS

1. Ibid., 57.

2. Hunt, *A History of the Sisters of St. Francis of the Holy Cross*, 17.

3. Sister Pauline, diary and notes in the archives of the Sisters of St. Francis, Bay Settlement, Wisconsin, as quoted in Shallow, *The Shrine of Our Lady of Good Help*, 57.

4. Shallow, *The Shrine of Our Lady of Good Help*, 57.

5. Ibid.

6. Ibid.

7. Shallow, *The Shrine of Our Lady of Good Help*, 59.

8. Author interview with Sr. Jeanne Jarvis, OSF, October 2, 2019.

9. Author interview with Sr. Mary Urban Schumacher, October 2, 2019.

10. Shallow, *The Shrine of Our Lady of Good Help*, 60.

11. Archives, Diocese of Green Bay, Chronology: Chapel at Robinsonville 1830-2001.

12. Ibid.

13. Shallow, *The Shrine of Our Lady of Good Help*, 60.

14. Author interview with Sr. Joanne Goessl OSF, October 2, 2019.

15. Corrie Campbell, "Franciscan roots run deep at Our Lady of Good Help Shrine," *The Compass*, April 19, 2019, 13A.

16. Shallow, *The Shrine of Our Lady of Good Help*, 69.

17. Sam Lucero, "Shrine Celebrates 160th anniversary in 2019," *The Compass*, April 19, 2019, 3A.

18. Author interview with Fr. John Girotti, July 17, 2018.

**Chapter Thirteen: WHAT DOES
THIS MEAN FOR US?**

1. Hope Bollinger, "Interesting Facts About the Meaning & Importance of the Number 12 in the Bible," https://www.crosswalk.com /faith/bible-study/12-interesting-facts-about-number-12-in-the-bible. html.

2. Known as the Great Famine or the Irish Potato Famine, that occurred in Ireland from 1845 to 1849. Blight caused crop failures by destroying the leaves and tubers of the potato plants. Potatoes were the primary food source for the Irish people, most of whom were tenant farmers and lived meagerly. About one million people died of starvation or starvation-related diseases. Encyclopedia Britannica, "Great Famine," https://www.britannica.com/event/Great-Famine-Irish -history.

3. The Miracle Hunter, "Messages of the Apparitions," http:// www.miraclehunter.com/marian_apparitions/messages/lasalette _messages.html.

4. The Miracle Hunter, "The Messages of Lourdes," http://www .miraclehunter.com/marian_apparitions/messages/lourdes _messages.html.

5. Weyant, Gillian, "The Top Catholic Pilgrimage Places in the World," CoraEvans.com, https://www.coraevans.com/blog/article /the-top-catholic-pilgrimages-in-the-world.

6. The Miracle Hunter, "The Messages of Fátima," http://www .miraclehunter.com/marian_apparitions/messages/fatima _messages.html.

7. "Rwanda genocide of 1994," Encyclopedia Britannica, https:// www.britannica.com/event/Rwanda-genocide-of-1994.

8. The Miracle Hunter, "The Message of Kibeho," http:// miraclehunter.com/marian_apparitions/messages/kibeho_messages .html.

9. Edward Looney, in correspondence with the author, April 20, 2021.

10. Michael O'Neill, in correspondence with the author, April 17, 2021.

11. David L. Ricken, Diocese of Green Bay, Wisconsin, in correspondence with the author, June 4, 2021.

12. Ibid.

About the Author

Marge Steinhage Fenelon is an award-winning author and journalist and internationally known speaker. She is the author of several books on Marian devotion and Catholic spirituality and is a popular Catholic media personality, having appeared numerous times on Relevant Radio, Ave Maria Radio, EWTN, and elsewhere. She blogs for *National Catholic Register* and on her website, MargeFenelon.com. She is an instructor for the Archdiocese of Milwaukee Deacon Wives Program as well. Her lively podcast, *Simply Holy*, airs on Breadbox Media. Marge and her husband grew up in Wisconsin where they raised their family and currently live.